A ROYAL CONSPIRACY

A ROYAL CONSPIRACY

Parallels between Princess Diana and Duchess Meghan

Courtney Hargrove

One Moment Books

Published by ONE MOMENT BOOKS

For information, address OneMomentBooks@Outlook.com

For the innocent ones. May you stay safe and protected.

TABLE OF CONTENTS

ABOUT THE AUTHOR

Courtney Hargrove is the pen name of a writer who covered royals, breaking news and celebrities during a twenty-plus-year journalism career working in nine countries.

Her time up close to the goings-on at various royal residences, including reporting on Kate Middleton, Prince William, Prince Harry, Meghan, the Duchess of Sussex, Princess Eugenie and Beatrice among others lends Hargrove's work the weight of authenticity and displays a true knowledge of the history of how this family relates to one another—and to outsiders.

She covered the wedding of King Charles III and Camilla Parker-Bowles in Windsor and has spent time up close with various British royals through work and...well... she believes pretty much everything Meghan and Harry say about them.

AUTHOR'S NOTE

First, I want to start with some content warnings for readers.

In the context of the history of the British monarchy, this book mentions: Sexual assault; rape; executions; beheadings; children in peril and discussion of child murder; drug injections; pedophilia; aliens; and bullying.

Equally important, this book is not for diehard monarchists. If you view the British royal family through the gauzy fairy-tale filter they drape over themselves, or see them as an unimpeachable entity made up of people who work occasionally yet are entirely deserving of their unearned riches and a position in life handed to them through hereditary entitlement, this book is not for you.

It is a no-holds-barred, unflinching look at some of the ways in which an institution has ensured its own survival with methods that are not always palatable nor laudable.

This book takes a laser-focused look at what the stakes are now, and how the very survival of the monarchy might be important enough to the family to prompt more desperate behavior in the coming years now that the steady and widely respected captain of their ship, Queen Elizabeth II, is no longer at the wheel.

Furthermore, you do not have to be a fan of the Sussexes, of Meghan and/or Harry, nor do you have to feel sorry for the wealthy and attractive pair, to acknowledge how they are targeted for supposed transgressions that remain unclear.

Neither Harry nor Meghan have asked anyone to feel sorry for them; they simply want the harassment, misinformation and overblown media coverage to stop. I don't think that's too much to ask in a world where hate seems to infuse every part of our lives now.

You have been warned.

Courtney Hargrove
October 8, 2022

CONSPIRACY

1. noun, plural con·spir·a·cies.
2. the act of conspiring
3. an unlawful, harmful, or evil plan formulated in secret by two or more persons; plot
   a combination of persons for such an unlawful, harmful, or evil purpose: He joined the conspiracy to overthrow the government.

Law.

4. an agreement by two or more persons to commit a crime, fraud, or other wrongful act.
5. any concurrence in action; combination in bringing about a given result.

CHAPTER 1

ROBOTS AND REPTILES: A CONSPIRACY TO DEHUMANIZE OUTSIDERS

It was June of 2018, and Meghan Markle and Prince Harry were newlyweds and freshly anointed the Duke and Duchess of Sussex by Queen Elizabeth II.

As an American and a former actress, Meghan had taken to the role of a senior working royal with grace and aplomb.

She was a beautiful and hard-working woman who seemed to make a lovely addition to the House of Windsor, and royal watchers worldwide were already on the lookout for a baby, which couldn't be far off, fans speculated.

Or could it?

In June, sharp-eyed fans saw something very suspicious that called into question the very existence of the human person we know as "Meghan Markle."

A disturbing video clip circulated all over the media that month. The 16-second video appeared to show a stone-faced, immovable, dead-eyed royal couple waving robotically from an audience packed with other live people.

Indeed, as the camera panned over Meghan and Harry in the audience, viewers saw an eerie imitation of what two humans should look like.

In one version of the video clip, "Pink Soldiers," a song from the Korean Netflix drama "Squid Game," played in the background. (This touch was added later when the clip made the rounds again in 2021).

"She is a Clone or something," a caption on the video read. "Our ruling world is sick."

Thus the Meghan-Markle-is-a-Robot narrative was cemented into the pantheon of British royal conspiracy theories.

How could we have missed it?

How could we not have seen it all along?

Harry and Meghan were applauding, but their faces were immovable. They were unblinking. They did not look human.

Ah, but that's because the faces *weren't* human!

"Meghan and Harry" were reportedly two humans wearing carefully crafted masks in the audience during the *Britain's Got Talent* TV show finale that year. It was all a stunt meant to promote the Live Figures exhibit at Madame Tussauds in London.

They were good likenesses.

Too good, in fact, according to many suspicious viewers.

So good, in fact, that the Associated Press wire service wrote an entire article debunking it. This was the set-up:

"CLAIM: Meghan, Duchess of Sussex, appears to be a clone or a robot in a video shared on Facebook.

AP'S ASSESSMENT: Missing context. This video shows a moving figure in a special exhibit years ago at Madame Tussauds wax museum in London. It does not show the real Meghan."

Despite this convincing evidence, the conspiracy theory remains, and people will still claim Meghan is not a human person.

Interestingly, there are those who still believe Meghan is real but who also suspect she is being used as a pawn in the British royal family's bid for world domination.

This particular group believes Harry married her as part of a grand plan, one involving the royal family playing a very long game.

The theory was popularized on November 27, 2017, the day Meghan and Harry announced their engagement.

That day, a wise observer suggested their union was the perfect way for Britain, which lost the Revolutionary War and has had it rubbed in their faces since the Declaration of Independence was signed in 1776, to take back the United States.

This plan is in place because the British never got over their loss, according to the late Greg Pollowitz, once the editor of the conservative news aggregator site twitchy.com.

He pointed out that Meghan's American citizenship meant Harry and Meghan's children could be U.S. president *and* one day ascend the British throne (that is, as long as Charles, William, George, Charlotte, Louis, Harry and Co are somehow out of the picture by then).

"Brits are playing long-ball here, but it's a smart move," Pollowitz wrote. "They want America back and this is how they'll do it."

With that Tweet, he set off a domino effect of conspiracy theories and breathless claims that Meghan's appearance on the scene was, indeed, part of England's plan all along.

Long before Meghan was a member of the royal family, Princess Diana was dealing with their special brand of strangeness.

It must have been an extremely odd week for the young teacher, for example, when, for seven days in the summer of 1981 before she was to marry Prince Charles, Diana was taken to a ritual at Clarence House in London.

There, the royal-wife-to-be was dressed in white and shown "who the Windsors really are."

In attendance with Diana were the Queen Mother, Queen Elizabeth II, Prince Philip, Lady Fermoy, Diana's father Earl Spencer, Prince Charles and Camilla Parker-Bowles, according to conspiracy theorist David Icke, who at one point in his career only wore turquoise shell suits.

At that ritual, according to Icke, who is best known for his belief that world leaders from the American Bush political dynasty to the British royal family are in fact seven-foot tall, blood-drinking reptilians, "Diana was told that she should consider her union with Prince Charles as only a means to produce heirs and nothing else. Camilla Parker-Bowles was his consort, not her. Prince Philip and the Queen Mother then shape-shifted into reptiles to show Diana who they really were. 'Diana was terrified, but quiet', she said. Diana was told that if she ever revealed the truth about them, she would be killed."

Icke added, "It is clear that Diana knew about the true nature of the royal family's genetic history and the reptilian control. Her nicknames for the Windsors were 'the lizards' and 'the reptiles' and she used to say in all seriousness: 'They're not human.'

"There is a very good reason for Diana using this description of the Windsors." (Icke is also a former sports broadcaster and alleged anti-Semite who had his visa revoked by Australia in 2019 for his Holocaust denial views; he denies being anti-Semitic or a Holocaust denier).

Over the years, it has been reported that Diana confidante Christine Fitzgerald, too, shared that the princess told her the royal family is made up of shape-shifting alien reptiles.

Wild as it sounds, the shape-shifting reptilian world leaders theory has endured since the 1990s. It has a fair number of believers and followers, maybe because it's not just the British royals who are in on the shape-shifting.

You know a conspiracy is capturing hearts and minds when it survives from the last century all the way to TikTok in the year 2022.

"The queen and Prince Philip are not human," says the speaker in a TikTok video shared Sept. 8 on Facebook while text runs over it: "reptilian queen of England" and "the queen is reptilian."

If you find yourself having doubts, media watchdog Poynter Institute can set you straight: "We rate these posts pants on fire!" their post debunking the reptile claims said.

The idea is that the royals' true identities as shape-shifting reptiles explains why they're so precious about their bloodlines.

Of course, the reasoning for that theory is actually *true*, and it's why so many of them have married their cousins over the years, which is why the family shrub is a few branches short of a tree.

To name a few: George V and Queen Mary were second cousins. George IV and Caroline were first cousins, as were Queen Victoria and King Albert, whose great-grandchildren would also marry each other—they were third cousins Queen Elizabeth II and Prince Philip.

The list goes on.

These are only a small dose of the outrageous claims surrounding people who find themselves in the grip of the British royal family.

Diana and her posthumous daughter-in-law Meghan have both been the subject of conspiracy theories, though at this writing Diana is far in the lead due to how many decades she has been in our hearts, and how she died so young and under such tragic, senseless circumstances.

Both women have received a befuddling amount of criticism over the years for transgressions that remain unclear.

Like Meghan, it seemed Diana's biggest offenses involved revealing the harm that was done to her while within the royal family.

The Princess of Wales is still vilified in some corners by those who believe the people and institutions who hurt Diana were never the problem; Diana's *sharing information* about the harm done to her was.

In high-society Britain, it appears the airing out of dirty laundry is far more distasteful than soiling that laundry in the first place.

It is a twisted reality that remains today. Victims who identify and seek justice from those who have hurt, harassed or assaulted them are dragged and abused on social media and even in mainstream media, while the offenders themselves seem to get away scot-free much of the time.

We can observe this in the way that Meghan talking about racism within the royal family and sharing the way in which her son Archie's skin tone was questioned before he was even born is the problem.

The priority is not rooting out the racism.

Rather, the focus is on punishing the ones who point it out.

In researching the bizarre and occasionally delusional narratives spun by and for bored conspiracy theorists, I began to wonder if such wild imaginings as these actually serve the royal family.

The more outrageous and fantastical and baseless the stories about robots, reptiles, fake pregnancies or Prince Philip conspiring to have Diana killed, the more these fake claims can serve to cloak, distract from or discredit actual scandals and alleged conspiracies that surface around the British royal family.

As long as we're busy talking about alien lizards, things that are really going on—suitcases of cash from powerful foreign billionaires, the "invisible contract" between the royal family and the media that cover them, or payoffs to rape accusers, for example—seem less intriguing somehow.

Less noteworthy. Less likely to be pursued on YouTube and picked apart on Twitter.

Take rumors that King Charles III is a vampire.

He leaned into that dramatic, nonsensical claim with his whole chest when he happily connected himself to vicious medieval dictator in a 2011 interview.

"Transylvania is in my blood," Charles, who was still a prince at the time, said. "The genealogy shows that I'm descended from Vlad the Impaler, you see."

Vlad, so-nicknamed because he liked to impale people on sticks and metal bars and other long hard things, became a legend for his sheer cruelty, and he was said to be the inspiration for Bram Stoker's Dracula.

Vlad tortured untold numbers of people, and under his rule an estimated 20,000 victims were once impaled and put on display outside the city of Targoviste.

This guy is related to the British royal family. There are modern connections, too: Charles owns a home in Transylvania, where Vlad's old house, Bran castle, remains a thriving tourist destination.

The House of Windsor's familial ties to the 15th-century ruler can be traced to Mary of Teck, grandmother of Charles's mother, the late Queen Elizabeth II. Mary was queen during the reign of King George V and was a Wurttemberg princess.

She was also believed to be descended from two of Vlad's sons, according to CBS news. King Charles is still drawn to his ancestral lands, and has been known to work to conserve the forests in Romania.

Despite this preponderance of circumstantial evidence, Charles is almost certainly not a vampire.

In any case, when it comes to outsiders, particularly women, the ugly rumors proliferate like viruses.

There are other harmful claims about both Diana and Meghan, and they live on because where there are wealthy, powerful, glamorous people, there is scrutiny.

There are lies and fantastical tales spun to pass the time or try to explain why these people are rich and famous and you're not.

In the course of my research for this book I came across claims more preposterous and baseless than the next, and I found these conspiracy theories further dehumanize these women and open the door just that little bit more to allow ridicule and misinformation to spread, and to make it seem OK.

Princess Diana was not killed because she was telling people the royal family were blood-guzzling lizard people.

Duchess Meghan is not a robot. (I can't believe I have to say this).

Both women were and are all too human, which made them all too vulnerable when they married into a powerful bloodline for love.

And if we eschew the robots and reptiles, we are left with the reality of conspiracies, violence and machinations that litter the past of the British monarchy.

The institution of the British monarchy has a long history of handling those people who prove inconvenient to them—or more dangerous still, those who pose an existential threat to them—without mercy.

What's to say the modern monarchy and courtiers are not as mercurial and prone to tactical operations as any family that sat on the British throne before them?

The same bloodlines that have occupied the castles and palaces for centuries will certainly have the same impulse for self-protection and self-preservation.

If truly under existential threat, there's no telling what an organism with an inbred survival instinct will do. How far will they go?

Time after time it has been shown that when they are under threat, the monarchy will fight, and they will fight hard.

With a brutally bleak economic picture in Britain, the pound sterling plummeting to historic lows, the #CostofLivingCrisis a relentless social media hashtag, the queen and matriarch of a nation dead and her out-of-touch son already sparking #KingCharlestheCruel labels, and growing cries to abolish the monarchy altogether, everything is converging at once against the royals.

The stakes haven't been so high in a very long time.

The question, how far will they go to ensure their own survival?

CHAPTER 2

A DUCHESS IN DANGER?

By the time the British Airways Airbus 777 from London's Heathrow touched down in Cape Town, South Africa, a legion of security teams, local police and airport ground crew were in place on the tarmac.

Inside the aircraft, a group of VIPs were ushered out of their seats so they could disembark first after a twelve-hour redeye.

Meghan, the Duchess of Sussex, held her four-month-old son Archie tight and waited for the airplane doors to open. With her was her husband Prince Harry, the Duke of Sussex, and their nanny, Lauren.

Meghan's mind was pacing through all she had to do that day. She was a tired new mom, still breastfeeding regularly, and had landed in a new time zone.

The first-time parents would have to help little Archie acclimatize, help him adjust both his sleep and eating patterns, while working virtually full time on this trip.

The Sussexes had come to South Africa for an official royal tour. Both Harry and Meghan intended to make their days count and planned to truly connect with every event they attended and every person they visited, no matter how tired they were, no matter how packed their schedules.

The working royals were determined to represent the British royal family with dignity and unrelenting work ethic.

The aircraft doors opened and Meghan and Harry smiled a greeting to all those who waited for them.

Though the local media in Cape Town had not been alerted to their precise plans, fellow travelers and passersby at the airport that day found themselves graced with serendipity and snapped photos and videos of the family as they descended the stairs.

Meghan, hair slicked back in a neat bun, smiled warmly and waved at everyone who'd gathered to greet them and whisk them safely to the British High Commissioner's sprawling residence.

She kept a firm grip on her son. This wasn't the Sussexes' first flight with baby Archie, but it was by far the longest, and he was doing wonderfully.

The baby squinted in the sun, kept warm in a white beanie with a pompom bouncing on top, one startlingly reminiscent of a hat placed on the head of Harry as an infant when he was photographed being carried off a plane by his mother Princess Diana in the 1980s.

As the Sussex entourage was escorted to their transport and driven to their South African base at the British High Commissioner's sprawling residence, they talked through how they'd hit the ground running once Archie and his nanny were settled in.

Fresh off a relaxing Mediterranean summer break with friends—first Ibiza, Spain, and then a break in the south of France—the Duke and Duchess had done their best to rest and relax, as much as new parents can with an infant to look after.

They stayed positive and had already done some of the homework necessary to learn who they'd be meeting on this whirlwind tour.

Once they arrived at their accommodations, they made sure Archie had enough to eat—Meghan was still breastfeeding, and would be taking nursing breaks in between official engagements in the coming days—and that Lauren was comfortable in the unfamiliar surroundings.

Before long, they would be racing out the door for their first engagement.

Harry and Meghan were ready to work, braced for the crowds to encompass them and seek their attention.

They had no way of knowing what was coming, and just how strong they would have to be to get through that tour.

Meghan and Harry left Archie with Lauren at the home that would be hosting the family in those first few days and departed as part of a security convoy to their first engagement.

It would be both an inspirational and sobering visit to Nyanga Township. At the time, media in South Africa often referred to Nyanga as "the murder capital" of the country.

As a lifelong fierce advocate for women and girls' rights, this trip was close to Meghan's heart.

She dressed for a relaxed atmosphere, donning a black-and-white print maxi wrap dress by Myamiko (a fair trade brand from Malawi, one of the countries Harry was planning to visit) with black Castañer wedges, and pulled her hair back in a sleek pony.

Upon arrival, the Sussexes were greeted by a group of young people who immediately drew them into the revelry. Meghan danced next to Harry, taking the hands of the local young people, smiling, and gamely following their lead.

They soon got down to serious business.

They were there to listen to the people who had come to meet them, including children, discuss their work of educating children about their rights as well as empowering young girls through self-defense classes.

The township was a place fighting a losing battle with femicide, so much so that the high violence and murder rate of women and girls had been declared a "national crisis."

When the meet and greet portion of the engagement was over, Meghan stepped up onto a tree stump to address the crowd, offering powerful words for an occasion that called for empathy and understanding.

"While I'm here as a member of the royal family, I stand here before you as a mother, a wife, a woman, as a woman of color and as your sister," she said.

The crowd clapped and cheered. If you stepped back just a little bit from the cameras, you would have seen a heavy security presence keeping watch.

Harry then stepped up, took his place on the stump, and spoke. "I wanted to ensure that our first visit as a family, with my wife by my side, focused on the significant challenges facing millions of South Africans while acknowledging the hope we feel so strongly here," he said.

He added, "No man is born to cause harm to women. This is learned behavior, and we need to break that cycle. My role is to defend my wife and be a positive role model for my son."

They each received raucous applause and melted under the innocent gazes of small children looking for their own role models. There were hugs all around.

As soon as they made it to their vehicles, Meghan's thoughts turned to Archie. Was he sleeping well? Would she need to squeeze in time to nurse him before her next engagement, which was coming up that very afternoon?

After a quick lunch and a wardrobe change, Meghan and Harry once again left Archie with Lauren and traveled to their next engagement, this time to the District Six Museum, which documents the destruction in a residential area of inner-city Cape Town that took place during apartheid.

Then, finally, they got to spend time with Archie, playing, singing, reading to him and getting a good night's sleep.

They'd need it.

Meghan and Harry hit the ground running the next morning, Sept. 24, and headed straight to Monwabisi Beach in their high-security convoy of SUVs and police vehicles.

There, along the stunning South African coastline, they would meet more young people working to change the world for the better.

The Sussexes are partial to these events, where the bright-eyed new generation facing existential climate crises speak to them with some nerves, yes, but also with a precocious determination that resonates with the activist couple who, despite many attempts by columnists and critics to paint them as courting attention for their own gain, enjoy shedding their celebrity skin when they can.

Beach-side in South Africa was the perfect place to do this.

Their hair and their clothes blew around them in windy conditions as they met with charities including Waves for Change and the Lunchbox Fund, which provides meals to children in townships and rural areas.

Once again Meghan and Harry were hugging and joking with local children and perhaps most important of all, they were listening.

The Sussexes conversed and joined in and blended, their natural warmth and genuine interest rendering the young people instantly comfortable, and gamely answered questions about being new parents.

They each made a point of complimenting each others' skills. Harry said Meghan is "the best mum," and Meghan returned the sentiment, confirming Harry is "the best dad."

Around the same time the tired parents were showing support for one another's parenting proficiency in Monwabisi Beach, Lauren had gotten the lay of the land of the property they were staying at back in Cape Town.

Archie was due for nap during the window when his parents were working, and his beloved nanny was cooing and rocking and winding him down to help shift him into sleep mode.

It was past time, but right before Lauren was about to lay the boy in his crib to (fingers crossed) fall easily and peacefully asleep, a thought popped into her head.

Something told her to head down to the kitchen to grab a snack first.

Something inexplicable.

Lauren listened to that voice in her head, and she scooped Archie up and padded downstairs.

The trained childcare professional hailed from Zimbabwe, and her employers have spoken of their appreciation for her way of carrying their son with a mud cloth, or a "bogolan," a hand-woven textile originating from Mali and decorated with patterns and symbols using only natural dyes, including aged river mud.

Meghan once remarked, "We loved that she would always tie him on her, on her back with a mud cloth."

And so Archie was snuggled up close to Lauren with her mud cloth as she made her way through the home in search of a bite of food.

When the Monwabisi Beach engagement was over, a throng of security, both uniformed and in plainclothes, ushered the Sussexes to their vehicles once again.

This time the couple split up. Harry's convoy was headed to Kalk Bay for an engagement with the Cape Town Maritime Police Unit and the Royal Marines, of which he had been appointed Captain General by Queen Elizabeth II in 2017.

His vehicle sped off toward the harbor where he would catch a ship out to sea in the direction of Seal Island, a poaching hot spot for the endangered abalone, a problem the prince would be learning all about that afternoon.

Meanwhile, Meghan, who was still breastfeeding and was fitting in feedings between engagements, hopped in her own SUV for another visit without Harry.

But as Meghan strapped in and the driver hit the gas, an aide delivered some shocking news: There had been a fire at the house—and it originated in the room Archie was staying in.

Meghan could hardly absorb the information. "What?" She replied, then echoed the cry: "What?"

The aide repeated the news as the SUV raced toward the high commissioner's mansion where the Sussex family was reportedly staying: "There's been a fire in the baby's room."

A member of the security entourage behind them at that moment recalls, "We were driving in convoy and all of a sudden, the convoy with Meghan broke away. We followed after…We weren't sure what was going on.

"The prince [Harry] was on his way to Kalk Bay for a thing with the [Marines]," the source told South African publication *The Citizen*.

What was "going on" was Meghan was beside herself.

Her role as mom was her number one priority, and her baby was in trouble.

Like a scene from a movie, the vehicle came to a halt and Meghan had the door open almost before the wheels stopped moving.

It appeared she was in a blind panic, sources reveal.

Said one witness, "I can tell you that she didn't get out of the car like a lady that normally gets out. She bolted into the house."

When Meghan made contact with Lauren, she found their "amazing nanny" in "floods of tears." She also discovered there was no smoke detector.

Lauren explained she had gone down for a snack before putting Archie down, which is when the heater in the nursery began burning and smoking, according to various accounts.

As Meghan hugged her baby, she learned it was sheer coincidence someone "happened to just smell smoke down the hallway, went in, fire extinguished," the duchess would later recall.

She said it several times, during and after the event: My baby was "supposed to be sleeping in there."

It was a chilling thought that brought on a feeling of doom: Her baby had escaped something that could have gone either way.

Meghan observed everyone involved was in tears and "shaken" by the incident, but in the midst of it she was prompted to get ready to go by royal aides, because she had another scheduled engagement.

The duchess resisted.

She asked her handlers and staff that had traveled with her to South Africa to rethink the day's events and perhaps move the schedule around.

"Can you just tell people what happened?"* Meghan implored, sure that everyone involved, including those preparing for their scheduled visits, would understand.

The answer seemed to be to strongly encouraging that "the show must go on."

And go on it did.

Editor's note: The palace nor the Sussexes' communications department have confirmed when this event occurred, and there are conflicting reports from sources, media reports and varying memories about the exact timing of this event, which happened years before it was publicly revealed. After investigating all sides of the events of that day, we felt the weight of the reporting indicated it likely occurred on Sept. 24.

It wasn't until three years later, in August of 2022, that Meghan revealed what went on that day in Archie's nursery.

During her debut Spotify podcast Archetypes, the duchess told her first guest—fellow mom, close friend and tennis champion Serena Williams—that "even though we were being moved to another place afterwards, we still had to leave [Archie] and go do another official engagement."

Meghan didn't want to rush off as quickly as she did.

But she complied, and in her podcast she suggested her royal handlers cared more about optics than a mother's concern.

"The focus ends up being on how it looks instead of how it feels," she said. "And part of the humanizing and the breaking through of these labels and these archetypes and these boxes that we're put into is having some understanding on the human moments behind the scenes that people might not have any awareness of and to give each other a break. Because we did—we had to leave our baby."

For Meghan, the events of that day peeled away one more layer of her feeling of safety. That moment robbed her just a little bit more of her autonomy and chipped away at the expectation she'd be treated like a person, not simply an extension of a family with its own agenda.

For those who don't believe there is a default setting in the British media to paint Meghan as a liar, opportunist and general detriment to the royal family need only witness the "gotcha"-style pieces that emerged within hours of the podcast dropping.

"Royal sources do not recall a 'fire' in baby Archie's hotel room during Meghan and Harry's South Africa tour," The *Daily Mail* UK Twitter account blasted to 700,000 followers out within hours of the revelation.

"Meghan's story of Archie escaping fire disputed by royal sources," the *Mercury News* of Silicon Valley's headline read.

The default is to fact-check an American woman of color who dares to speak.

If Kate Middleton had uttered any combination of words about a threat to her children, there would have been a race to ratchet up the drama with her as the central heroine.

News outlets would have blasted out content and headlines so sympathetic you couldn't help but squeeze out tears for the Duchess of Cambridge. There would be no questioning or suspicion. No minimizing or attempts to debunk Kate's words.

The British press would have fallen all over themselves to find anyone and everyone who could attest to how much danger the Cambridge children had been in. I know how it works. I used to do that kind of newsgathering myself.

You don't have to like or care about Meghan Markle to acknowledge this behavior by certain corners of the media, nor do you have to feel sorry for the wealthy and beautiful duchess. All that is required is a clear-eyed view of how Kate is treated versus how Meghan is.

Kate is rewarded for sitting still, staying quiet, and looking pretty.

Meghan is vilified for existing.

In any case, the British media got down to work trying to debunk the nursery fire claims, but in the end managed only to minimize them.

"Others are understood to recall the incident…and while they do not remember there actually being a fire, the heater was certainly smoking and was unplugged and dealt with," read one tabloid article.

The *Mercury News* story went straight for the misogynistic language: "Critics of the Duchess of Sussex, including royal biographer Angela Levin, suggest that this story could be another example of how the former TV actress can be an unreliable narrator."

Indeed, after the podcast revelation, Levin jumped in with her two cents, writing, "Meghan outraged that she had to go on another royal engagement in South Africa after she heard there was a fire in baby Archie's room. Nasty to hear but as an actress doesn't she know the show must go on. Luckily he wasn't there but odd it was never leaked to the press."

A tabloid reporter then wrote, "royal sources confirmed to the *Daily Mail* that there was an incident involving a heater at the High Commissioner's residence… but they say it didn't happen the way Meghan described."

Here's where a particular aspect of the conspiracy comes into play: There was no official comment from any of the various palaces—Buckingham, Kensington or otherwise (the Queen was still alive and ruling when Meghan shared her story)—but The Firm was leaking like a sieve.

"I'm told Buckingham Palace aides were most definitely not keeping calm, nor carrying on after the [podcast] premiere on Tuesday, worried about what else might be shared over the next twelve weeks," royal reporter Omid Scobie wrote on Yahoo!. "Two aides have already pushed back on Meghan's 'precise recollection' of events in South Africa—one told a tabloid that it was a smoking heater, not a fire (does it matter?) and **another claimed it is 'unfair' to share such stories when the Royal Household cannot comment.**" (Emphasis mine).

Did you catch that? Palace aides, who run the royal household, are complaining the palace is treated unfairly by Meghan because they can't comment—*while they are making comments to the media.*

The royals indeed briefed their preferred tabloids with the royal family's side of the fire story post haste; see previous above examples.

The royal households were not hamstrung as they'd have us believe.

They did not keep quiet.

Anyway, these "royal sources" agreed Harry and Meghan would have been expected to carry on with their engagements, but also briefed the media that as senior royals, the pair would have had the final say about whether to keep working.

The *Telegraph* newspaper added some context, quoting sources saying that had Meghan and Harry interrupted their schedules to stay with Archie for a bit longer, that there would have been concern that "news about the incident, or the sudden cancellation of events, would have overshadowed their work in South Africa."

It wasn't until the South African publication *The Citizen* confirmed there was a frightening and dangerous incident in Archie's nursery that the press reluctantly acknowledged Meghan's veracity.

In writing stories in which they begrudgingly acknowledged she told the truth, the British newspapers were also admitting they failed to confirm the story themselves, even given a full week to do so.

I've worked with them. If this had been Kate Middleton, she would've been coddled and possibly submitted for sainthood and raised up like a hero who'd singlehand-edly rescued a pack of babies and kittens from a burning orphanage.

"It is the first confirmation that a fire as reported in a podcast by Meghan Markle actually happened after the British Foreign, Commonwealth & Development Office refused to comment," the *Mail* wrote in its follow-up story a week later in reporting on *The Citizen's* scoop with their security source.

This source told all about the aftermath of the smoking heater:

"When we got to the house, the housekeeper called me and showed me the heater that was burnt and told me what had a happened and that the child was not in the room at the time the heater burnt, they smelt it, went up and saw the smoke," said the source, who added that the fire was not officially reported to authorities.

"When we were outside, we discussed what we are going to do about this. It was a new heater that was just purchased and the consensus was 'guys this is gonna look bad for us or for Cape Town, South Africa, or for whoever.'"

"The British Police guys actually told us 'guys just leave it as is, don't talk about this.'"

And thus, it was covered up.

The source says it was immediately decided the Sussex family could no longer live in the official residence.

"What was significant is, we immediately moved out of that house. But the second place, where they went to, was not even five minutes away from the official residence where we were stationed and none of us were told where they were staying after the fire," they added.

"We decided we are not going to expose this thing. That's why we kept quiet about it back then, because we knew we were going to get backlash."

All of this confirms what Meghan and Harry have been telling us for years. It shows how quickly the new mom was expected to gather herself and leave the feelings of terror behind—along with her baby.

The speed with which the palaces briefed the British media to deny, and then minimize, was another jab at Meghan and a way to attempt to discredit her lived experience.

We are intelligent people; we do not need a citing to understand how damaging smoke is to an infant's developing lungs. It does not take a blazing inferno to badly harm a child.

Here's a citing anyway:

"Breathing in hot air, smoke, or chemical fumes can cause irritation or swelling in your child's airways. Being in or near a fire can cause wheezing and breathing problems. Your child may not notice these problems until several hours later. When your child inhales smoke, harmful toxins may get into your child's body. This is more likely if the smoke came from burning plastics or synthetic materials."

(source: Canada government health services).

That, of course, is the outcome only if the intake is minimal.

Smoke inhalation is the leading cause of death related to fires. It ravages the body by any combination of asphyxiation (a lack of oxygen), chemical irritation, chemical asphyxiation, or even one alone can be deadly. To an infant's tiny, still-developing lungs, the effects of uncontrolled smoke are unthinkable.

There were no smoke detectors in the home.

No wonder Meghan and Harry were shaken to their cores.

The evening after it happened, the Duke and Duchess of Sussex concluded their second day in Cape Town with a reception at the British High Commissioner Nigel Casey's residence.

Hair flowing freely, a loose, relaxed maxi-dress swishing around her legs, Meghan continued to do as she was asked, and kept up appearances: Everything was just fine and dandy in the new royal couple's life.

Nothing to see here. She did what aides expected of her.

Thank you, next.

There is, of course, no suggestion the royal family had anything to do with the fire or the smoking heater in South Africa, whichever it was.

The incident was reported as an accident and no one has disputed that.

But evidence piled upon evidence compiled since Meghan has been a member of the family has many royal watchers, and certainly Sussex supporters, fans and members of the general population, pointing out dark similarities in the way she and Diana were treated by the institution of the British royal family.

Some of what are called coincidences in the life of Meghan and Diana do more than raise eyebrows.

It's enough to give you chills.

CHAPTER 3

THE PAST AND THE PRESENT COLLIDE

All of this leads us to the next piece of the conspiracy. Its two parts run parallel through time, punching through the wormhole, bringing the Duchess of Sussex and Diana, the Princess of Wales, side-by-side in history, though never close enough to touch.

They will forever be hurtling through space and time separately, enhancing Harry's life irrevocably and being his biggest supporters over decades.

Here's the important context: The royal family and their courtiers, the so-called men in grey suits running The Firm, knew something the rest of us didn't when they encouraged the Sussexes to keep to their schedule after Archie's nursery fire: Only weeks before, Meghan says she reported feelings of depression and had told The Firm she was struggling with her mental health.

COURTNEY HARGROVE

The duchess had kept smiling in public in her last weeks of pregnancy with Archie, but she wasn't OK—not at all.

The royal family, she and Harry maintain, knew this.

"I was really ashamed to say it at the time and ashamed to have to admit it to Harry, especially because I know how much loss he's suffered. But I knew that if I didn't say it, that I would do it," Meghan told Oprah in her and Harry's sweeping interview in 2021. "I just didn't want to be alive anymore, and that was a very clear and real and frightening constant thought."

Meghan says she asked for help from those who run the royal family, but was rebuffed because it might reflect badly on The Firm, as the palace courtiers and offices are colloquially referred to.

Still, the suicidal thoughts persisted during that dark time in 2019. "I thought it would have solved everything for everyone," Meghan said.

In an interview on that same South African tour in which she was wide-eyed and a bit shaky, Meghan would reveal some of her struggle.

"Any woman, especially when they're pregnant, you're really vulnerable, and so that was made really challenging. And then when you have a newborn, you know. And especially as a woman, it's a lot," she told the ITV documentary *Harry & Meghan: An African Journey*.

"So you add this on top of just trying to be a new mom or trying to be a newlywed. It's um…yeah. I guess, also thank you for asking because not many people have asked if I'm okay, but it's a very real thing to be going through behind the scenes."

Some in the British media mocked her for opening up, called her an "actress," said she was a terrible one, and gave little credence to her cries for help.

Others gave her the grace any one of us deserves in allowing a vulnerable moment to be recorded for posterity: She says she's in pain. Listen to her.

Meghan's husband wasn't putting up with any of it. He released a statement of his own in October of 2019 saying flat-out she was being targeted.

"Unfortunately, my wife has become one of the latest victims of a British tabloid press that wages campaigns against individuals with no thought to the consequences—a ruthless campaign that has escalated over the past year, throughout her pregnancy and while raising our newborn son," the statement read.

Ah, but who, in turn, was the media working with? Because they couldn't do it all alone.

Just like they couldn't 35 years ago when it was happening to Princess Diana.

CHAPTER 4

WAS DIANA WARNED ABOUT A CAR-CRASH CONSPIRACY?

The death of Princess Diana in 1997 spawned some of the most twisty and enduring conspiracy theories in modern history.

In the summer of 2022, interest in her story ratcheted up for a new generation—Generation X and earlier had already soaked up every detail of Diana's royal life and the aftermath of her death like it was happening in our own families—with the release of two new documentaries.

The first, *The Princess* on HBO, is an immersive, stark, unflinching look at Diana's life and evolution from teen-aged school teacher to royal wife to hounded divorcee and, ultimately, to her premature death at age 36.

The second program took a deep dive into the investigation with unprecedented cooperation from the most important figures in the story. *The Diana Investigations* docuseries ultimately seemed intent on disproving all the conspiracy theories that remained.

Though the French Brigade Criminelle completed their investigation in 1999, the world still wouldn't accept it was an accident.

British investigator Lord John Stevens was charged in 2004 with putting to rest all the theories, claims and fantastical guesses about what "really" happened that night in Paris.

He was meant to face head-on the unrelenting suggestions from the public and the media that the late Prince Philip and the British royal family ordered MI5 and MI6 to stage the car crash in Paris' Pont de l'Alma tunnel that killed Princess Di, her boyfriend Dodi Al-Fayed, and their body guard Henri Paul.

Fayed died instantly when their black Mercedes, speeding through the tunnel over 60 mph, slammed into a concrete pillar in the Alma underpass in Paris at 12:22 a.m. on Aug. 31, 1997.

Reports emerged that medics thought Diana might survive her injuries, but she died after being transported to the hospital.

Those who have shared their theories about what caused the crash from every corner of the world since the day Diana died have always been reluctant to believe it was an accident.

You can hardly blame them.

In a chilling portent of her own death, Diana said more than once that she believed certain people around her were planning to cause her death and make it look like an accident.

In 1993, not long after she and her husband Prince Charles formally separated, the princess wrote a note predicting her own death.

It wasn't until October 2003 that the letter became public, courtesy of her former butler Paul Burrell. UK tabloid the Daily Mirror published a photograph of the note, written in Diana's loopy scrawl:

"I am sitting here at my desk today in October, longing for someone to hug me and encourage me to keep strong and hold my head high," it reads in part. "This particular phase in my life is the most dangerous—my husband is planning 'an accident' in my car, brake failure and serious head injury in order to make the path clear for Charles to marry." (You can find the full note online).

Sometime royal reporter and author Duncan Larcombe told the 2022 Diana docuseries that when it came to light, Diana's letter "was a complete game changer, another missing piece of the jigsaw."

He added, "'Diana's fears that she'd be murdered,' that fits in with what [Mohammed] Al-Fayed said. It also fits in with the large flash [that witnesses saw in the tunnel that night]. Suddenly, you're joining the dots."

That wasn't all.

There was also the "Mishcon Note." This bombshell missive came precisely two years later, in October 1995, when Diana and her secretary Patrick Jephson sat in a private meeting with her legal advisor Victor Mishcon.

Mishcon took careful notes during the encounter, which happened months before Diana and Charles would finally divorce after a three-year official separation.

The lawyer wrote that his world-famous client told him "reliable sources" had informed her certain people were planning to "get rid of her" by staging a car accident that would either kill her, or even just to injure her and make her seem "unbalanced."

This attempt on her life, Diana reportedly said, would happen by April of 1996 and the preferred method would likely be a car accident caused by brake failure or other means.

"The most important thing about that report, and the wait-a-minute moment, light shining through the darkness suddenly, was the Mishcon Note," Michael Mansfield, an attorney who represented Mohamed Al-Fayed, the father of Dodi, says in the Diana docuseries. "The note had been put in a safe at the New Scotland Yard."

An investigator hired by Al-Fayed also trumpeted its importance, pointing out Diana was definitive in her word choice.

"She doesn't say: 'I dreamed.' She doesn't say: 'I think.' She says: 'I was warned,'" said Michel Kerbois. "'They want to have me killed in a car accident.' That's what happened."

Though the French authorities had already investigated the crash and closed their case, the conspiracy theories were only growing more fervent in the ensuing years.

The collective "they" were saying Diana and Dodi were deliberately killed, claimed that other vehicles had purposefully forced the Mercedes to swerve, and even accused Henri Paul of being in on it.

It was Dodi's father, sometime-billionaire and one-time owner of Harrod's Ritz hotels Mohammed Al-Fayed, who shouted the loudest about a royal conspiracy.

He said flat-out that senior members of the royal household were behind the fatal crash and named Prince Philip as the primary aggressor, saying they did it all because they didn't want Dodi to be the stepfather of the future king (Prince William).

Al-Fayed said he believed not only were Diana and Dodi engaged, but that she was pregnant; it has been shown definitively by medical records she was not expecting.

A friend told the British tabloid *The Sun* that "Mohamed remains confident that information will emerge confirming his belief that Dodi and Diana were deliberately killed by the security services…he believes that was because the Establishment would not allow a Muslim to be married to the woman who would be the mother of the future king."

In a written statement he read at the inquest, Al-Fayed added that the plan for the crash was "executed" by the British and French secret intelligence services, with help from the CIA.

When asked what evidence he had for all of his serious allegations he replied, "You want me to get the proof, but I am facing a steel wall from the security services."

The cacophony grew so loud, the fingers kept jabbing so furiously in Prince Philip's direction, that the British Metropolitan Police were instructed to begin their investigation in 2004.

They dubbed it Operation Paget. It was led by then-Metropolitan Police Commissioner John Stevens, and he and his team plowed through every loose end, every suspicious occurrence, every viable witness.

The role of the paparazzi has spawned its own conspiracy theories. If you check the CCTV footage of driver Henri Paul on the night of the crash you'll see that he's seen waving to photographers.

An Inspector Carpenter told the British inquest that one photographer sitting in his car near where Diana and Dodi would exit the Ritz hotel was in contact with other paparazzi across the road.

"You will see Henri Paul exit [at the back of the hotel] and when you watch this sequence you will see him raise his hand as if waving to the paparazzi across the road. If you look at the paparazzi you will see one of them raises his camera," Carpenter said, according to The Guardian.

Speculation was rife that someone in the hotel was tipping off the paparazzi about Diana's movements.

There was also speculation that a white Fiat Uno, which was believed to have collided with the Mercedes, was driven by a photographer. (That is no longer the favored theory).

Ah, the famous Fiat.

Unlike many other suspicious aspects of the crash that have been asked, answered and/or debunked, the Fiat remains shrouded in mystery.

Indeed, the car that is said to have been a close witness, if not an aggressor, in the legendary events of that night has never been found.

A couple at the scene saw a white Fiat Uno coming out of the tunnel with a driver who was focused on his mirrors, according to investigators.

The couple described seeing a man with short hair and a dog wearing a muzzle in the car. Traces of white paint were found on the dark Mercedes Diana was riding in, and its tail light was broken.

It was determined the Mercedes had "glancing contact" with the Fiat.

Fabrice Cuvillier, of France's Brigade Criminelle, says to this day that the Fiat Uno exists, telling the Diana investigation docuseries, "We did not find this Fiat. But it would be dishonest of me to look you in the eye and say 'we didn't let the Fiat Uno slip through.' I don't think so, but I'm not 100 percent sure.'"

French investigator Eric Gigou added, "In my mind the only door that remains open is the testimony of the driver of the Fiat Uno."

The findings of Operation Paget were unveiled in December 2006 and totaled 832 pages.

Lord Stevens spoke to young princes Harry and William before the Operation Paget findings were made public, when the princes were young adults in their early twenties, and he told them everything.

He relayed that to the best of his ability, he and his team had debunked every conspiracy theory.

Problem was, he left the princes with a fiercer distrust and disgust of the press and the photographers who fed the beast than ever.

Operation Paget's final end came with the coroner's inquest. It began in the autumn of 2007, and by spring, all the evidence had been heard, and the jury came to the verdict that Diana and Dodi were "unlawfully" killed as a result of "gross negligence" by the driver, Henri Paul, as well as the paparazzi who chased the car.

One can imagine William and Harry's anger at those who'd hounded their mother for so long up until the Mercedes hit that pillar in Paris.

The jury listening to the inquest cited contributing factors being Paul's impairment through alcohol, and the fact neither Diana nor Dodi were wearing a seatbelt. Had they strapped in, officials determined, there is a "probability" they would have survived the crash.

The inquest found the princess was unlawfully killed because driver Henri Paul was drunk and driving too fast, the car was being chased by photographers and that Diana and Dodi might have survived had they been wearing seatbelts.

Yet questions remain, and likely always will.

It's impossible to convince some people that Princess Diana's death was an accident, Lord Stevens says to this day.

Put simply, her fans couldn't handle the truth.

"She was so popular. People find it very difficult to understand how someone like that could die in such an accident," Stevens said. "You will have certain people around who—whatever the evidence—will still think there is a conspiracy here. I think it is probably impossible [to persuade them otherwise]."

Stevens explains that the investigation considered all 104 allegations surrounding Diana's death "including probing the origins and credibility of the Mishcon Note."

The top cop said he interviewed Mishcon "on three occasions and took further statements on that letter," admitting that "it's something that caused me great concern."

In fact, Stevens has said, he was in touch with the lawyer even into his last days: "I saw Lord Mishcon about a month before he died, in about the spring of 2005, and he held course to the fact that he thought she [Diana] was paranoid, and he hadn't held much credence to it. He was her solicitor, and remember, a solicitor has legal obligations to their clients."

Paranoid? Maybe.

But remember that saying? The one that feels particularly apt when talking about the British royals, and the one Diana clearly kept in mind in her last years on the fringes of that very powerful family?

It goes like this: Just because you're paranoid doesn't mean they're not out to get you.

Put another way, the problem with conspiracy theories is sometimes they turn out to be true.

CHAPTER 5

THE FIRM AND THE FAMILY

A key parallel between Diana and Meghan's lives is their shared experience with how The Firm runs the royal household—and how the two women were treated rather coldly by that side of the monarchy.

Many people have only a basic idea of what The Firm is, in that it's a label used colloquially to refer to the amorphous group we know as The British Royals.

In reality, there are two arms of the British monarchy.

Meghan put it plainly in the Oprah interview in 2021: "So, there's the family, and then there's the people that are running the institution," she said.

Exactly.

Meghan has always said she got along well with Queen Elizabeth, who "has always been wonderful to me."

But when Meghan went to the business arm of the royal institution for support, she was refused help, she says, because she isn't on the payroll.

The members of this side of the crown include the infamous "men in grey suits" Princess Diana told us about in decades past, those staffers and courtiers who watch over the royals' schedules and keep the Firm running as best they can.

The business side manages royal affairs from offices including the Private Secretary's Office, the Privy Purse and the Treasurer's Office. They oversee the king's government relations, as well as finances and human resources. This is what people mean when they refer to the Royal Household.

The Firm became the nickname for the business side of the crown, which employs hundreds of people. The name reportedly originated with King George VI's statement that he and the rest of the royals were "not a family, we're a firm."

The three men with the most influence are the principal private secretaries at Buckingham Palace, Clarence House and Kensington Palace, and it's known in royal-watcher circles that Meghan clashed with the Queen's private secretary, Sir Edward Young.

Author and royal commentator Robert Lacey revealed Diana and Meghan were onto something in side-eying the men in grey:

"The courtiers in the British system are the rulers of their masters and mistresses, they're not really underlings," Lacey has said, according to an article in the *Sydney Morning Herald*.

Diana used the phrase "men in grey" to describe those who ran things behind the scenes and did not, in her view, have her best interests at heart.

She felt they were watching her every move. As Diana's friend James Colthurst told the *Daily Mail*, she "constantly felt under pressure from 'grey men' who were a group of unnamed people believed to be representing establishment figures in the royal family. 'She often felt she was doing her bit for The Firm, as she called it, and she wasn't appreciated.'"

Meghan, years later, also spoke about the courtiers' particular brand of control with Oprah, who asked how she felt about the palace hearing her speak her truth.

"I don't know how they could expect that after all of this time **we would still just be silent if there's an active role that the firm is playing in perpetuating falsehoods about us** and if that comes with risk of losing things, there's a lot that's been lost already," Meghan replied. (Emphasis mine).

When that comment was aired, it brought up stark comparisons to Princess Diana in 1995 when she spoke of "the establishment" she married into.

Diana knew they viewed her as a "non-starter," or a person who would not be suitable to be queen consort one day, because "I do things differently, I don't go by a rule book and because I lead from the heart not the head…and albeit that's got me into trouble in my work, I understand that. But someone's got to go out there and love people and show it."

By the time the summer of 2022 rolled around, we were in a time of major global royal-related events that began to highlight the similarities between Meghan and Diana for many who hadn't noticed them before.

The struggles of the two women were beginning to strike a chord with royal watchers worldwide.

It was the 25th anniversary of Diana's tragic death in August; the statue unveiling at Kensington Palace in June; and both riveting documentaries (HBO and Discovery+) also in August.

It all dovetailed.

Diana and Meghan's fans overlap in many areas. It was rapidly becoming clear in that season of the year 2022 that the same people who adored Princess Diana for her service, warmth, and genuine connection to people also are drawn to Duchess Meghan for the same reasons.

And many have already realized how similar their treatment by the royal family has been.

CHAPTER 6

PROTECTING THEIR OWN

At the various public events surrounding the funeral of Queen Elizabeth II, the beloved and longest-reigning British sovereign of all time, there was a man walking front and center whose very appearance triggered people worldwide.

The man was Prince Andrew, the queen's alleged "favorite son."

He is an accused rapist and known associate of a convicted pedophile and human traffickers, had he had pride of place in the ceremonial events that ruled the first few weeks of September 2022.

For anyone offended by, touched by or suffering from sexual abuse, Prince Andrew is a walking reminder of the pain such assaults bring.

One could certainly find space to empathize and employ logic during that time to say Andrew lost his mother and deserved to mourn alongside his family.

But if you place his appearance in the greater picture of how he still fits in with an institution that thrives in part off of British taxpayers' money, and considering how vile Andrew's connection to the late Jeffery Epstein and now-jailed Ghislaine Maxwell is, his looming presence clearly reflected on other members of the family.

Thus, the issue was not so much that Andrew didn't have a right to mourn his mother alongside the rest of her family.

It was his visibility that rankled. His front-row place was a reminder of how much he was still cossetted by the royal family and how much of an important place he still held in it—even after he was connected to one of the most atrocious and inhumane criminal activities possible.

At this writing he remains a counselor of state on official business. The queen kept Andrew in the line-up of people who could stand in for her on the most important official business should the occasion arise, and King Charles III hasn't changed that (yet). What does that say about the family's priorities?

Andrew drew attention for unfortunate reasons during those funeral events.

Social media, particularly TikTok influencers, posted they were genuinely disgusted when Andrew was seen stroking his daughter's behind in front of cameras broadcasting globally while on a walkabout to see the flowers and notes left for his mother after her death.

As people online debated, with some saying it seemed entirely normal and was something done in passing, most seem to agree it was, at the very least, bizarre and creepy and appeared entirely avoidable; TikTok duly pointed out the *eww* factor.

One posted a video saying, "Is this right for Prince Andrew to put his hand on his daughter like this inappropriately like he has...he needs to be questioned, this is definitely a no-no."

Prince Andrew, who has always denied assaulting anyone, has still been a problem for the family by his sheer association with these criminals.

There was the video released of Andrew peeking out of Epstein's New York front door sheepishly as he says goodbye to a young woman.

There were articles and headlines like "Prince Andrew's toxic fixation: Since they met, the Duke of York and paedophile Jeffrey Epstein partied together at least 20 times—even after the financier was convicted" in the *Daily Mail*.

There was the Channel 4 (UK) documentary *The Prince & the Paedophile* that told viewers Epstein had 13 phone numbers for Prince Andrew in his address book.

Through it all, one of Epstein's sex trafficking victims, Virginia Giuffre, maintained that Prince Andrew assaulted her and said he "knows exactly what he's done, and I hope he comes clean about it."

There was the disastrous BBC interview Andrew did to try to distance himself from his pedophile friend.

Asked if he regretted his friendship with Epstein, the prince replied, "Now, still not, and the reason being is that the people that I met and the opportunities that I was given to learn either by him or because of him were actually very useful."

Viewers, understandably, leapt on that, as well as the fact Andrew called the pedophile sex-trafficker "Mr. Epstein" at one point.

His most striking gaffe in what some called a "bizarre" interview was when Prince Andrew claimed that his onetime pal, pedophile Jeffrey Epstein, "quite obviously conducted himself in a manner unbecoming."

The BBC's interviewer quickly snapped back, "*Unbecoming?* He was a sex offender!"

Social media went to town dragging, mocking and deriding the prince after that.

Through it all, when U.S. authorities were seeking his help to investigate claims of child rape, Prince Andrew's mother the queen didn't fade into the background and let him fight his own battles.

She engaged in what amounted to *a photo op* to display her very public backing of Andrew.

Queen Elizabeth II mounted her favorite horse and trotted along the countryside next to Andrew in a show of support and solidarity, and the next day the photos were all over the British newspapers and the internet.

Still, the pressure continued mounting on Andrew and the royal family.

Then came more fuel dumped on the dumpster fire. In the spring of 2021 there was a new looming scandal:

Meghan and Harry were sitting down for a tell-all interview with talk-show Queen Oprah Winfrey.

The royal family didn't have a clue what the couple would say, but their words would be broadcast globally, and the Firm clearly showed they wanted to get ahead of whatever it would be.

Someone told the UK's *Times* newspaper that Meghan, the Duchess of Sussex, was being investigated by the palace for "bullying," and these bullying claims were revealed by former royal aide Jason Knauf.

This big story was released days before the dreaded Oprah interview.

It doesn't seem a stretch to suggest a drama might have been manufactured and the timing of the "investigation's" leak designed to discredit the duchess, so whatever Meghan said in the interview would be side-eyed.

Which leads us to another frighteningly similar conspiracy in the lives of Diana and Meghan. The race to discredit the women, who clearly have valid concerns and complaints about life inside the British royal institution, has never stopped.

Back in the 1990s, after Diana and Charles announced they would divorce, Diana became a loose end no one knew what to do with.

The monarchy does not like loose ends.

Diana's own words in the famous fraudulently obtained BBC interview with disgraced journalist Martin Bashir echo down the years:

"I was the separated wife of the Prince of Wales, I was a problem, full stop. Never happened before, what do we do with her?"

Diana was beloved by citizens of nations around the globe.

She believed The Firm was taking a tack that was meant to attempt to reduce her popularity, thus reducing her influence and ability to defend herself as an outsider in a historically powerful family.

Case in point: Somehow, *somehow*, private phone calls and records of some of Diana's calls that came from inside her home at Kensington Palace were leaked to the rabid British media.

One narrative that emerged in the tabloids was about "obsessive" calls to a male friend which Diana said did not happen, and one flirty call with James Gibney, who Diana said was simply a friend.

"The implications of that conversation were that we'd had an adulterous relationship, which was not true," Diana said in the interview.

"Have you any idea how that conversation came to be published in the national press?" Bashir inquired.

Diana replied, "No, but it was done to harm me in a serious manner, and that was the first time I'd experienced what it was like to be outside the net, so to speak, and not be in the family."

Now we travel back to 2021, when Meghan Markle is served up as a problem for the British royal family.

Someone associated with the Firm leaked to the *Times* that Meghan was the subject of a bullying investigation stemming from 2018.

The timing struck many as extremely suspicious.

First, these explosive claims could serve to make Meghan look bad before her sit-down.

The *Times* reported a complaint was made against Meghan by a close aide, one that was revealed by the Sussexes' former communications secretary Jason Knauf. The gist was that Meghan made unreasonable demands that made two personal assistants quit and undermined a third staffer during Meghan's two-year period as a working royal.

Meghan and Harry's team hit back with a strong rebuttal, saying what many were already thinking: the claims were deliberately leaked ahead of the Oprah interview.

"Let's just call this what it is—a calculated smear campaign based on misleading and harmful information," a Sussex spokesperson said.

"The duchess is saddened by this latest attack on her character, particularly as someone who has been the target of bullying herself and is deeply committed to supporting those who have experienced pain and trauma. She is determined to continue her work building compassion around the world and will keep striving to set an example for doing what is right and doing what is good."

It didn't work, of course. Though the usual bots, trolls and racists—including those within the British media—came out to blast Meghan and Harry after the Oprah interview, by and large, we know now, the global response was hugely in the Sussexes' favor.

Still, the effect of releasing the bullying claims at that time had another job to do: they used Meghan's name to distract from the very real specter of Prince Andrew becoming embroiled in a lawsuit related to his friend, convicted pedophile Jeffrey Epstein.

Lawyers representing some of Epstein's victims spoke out when the bullying claims surfaced, and one could take away from their statements that the media's and the royal family's hyper-focus on Meghan, who was long gone from the hallowed palace halls, was a slap in the face to victims who were permanently traumatized by being sexually assaulted and trafficked—and were being virtually ignored.

Attorney Gloria Allred pulled no punches: "Why does Buckingham Palace not conduct an investigation and make a public statement condemning Prince Andrew for failing to provide what is requested to those who are seeking the whole truth and justice for the victims of crimes against children?" She said in a statement to DailyMail.com.

"Why has Prince Andrew not been stripped of the royal titles that he enjoys, as has been the case for Meghan and Harry? He has certainly not brought dignity and respect to his work as a royal," she added. (At the time of the statement, Andrew still held his titles and was not cooperating with FBI requests to speak with him).

Allred was advocating for Andrew to speak with U.S. criminal investigators over his ties to Epstein, who killed himself in his prison cell in 2019.

She also told the *Guardian* newspaper that "allegations about him [Andrew] are far worse than the allegations about Meghan Markle. Prince Andrew was a working royal when he became a friend of Jeffrey Epstein, who was a sexual predator...**the investigation into Meghan Markle is a distraction, and it appears hypocritical under the circumstances. I have to wonder if it reflects a calculated decision to take the focus off of Prince Andrew.**" (You guessed it—emphasis mine).

Allred went on, "In addition, it should immediately issue a statement condemning Prince Andrew for failing to provide full in-person cooperation in the ongoing criminal investigation by the United States justice department."

Her daughter, lawyer Lisa Bloom, who also represented Epstein victims, told DailyMail.com in a statement: "Prince Andrew has long been accused of sexual misconduct toward a teenaged girl, and there is no question that he befriended prolific predator Jeffrey Epstein, even flying out to visit him in person after Epstein was released from jail.

"Where is Buckingham Palace's condemnation of that behavior? Where is its investigation of him? Investigating Meghan Markle only for far more minor complaints proves her point: that she has been singled out for unfair special treatment."

Only a few months after the interview and ensuing kerfuffle, in August of 2021, Virginia Giuffre filed suit, accusing Prince Andrew of sexual assault and rape in the first and third degree when she was 17.

Her lawyers alleged that the Prince sexually assaulted her three times, once in London, again in New York, and a third time on Epstein's private island in the U.S. Virgin Islands. Andrew denied all allegations against him.

Not long after a judge rejected Andrew's legal team's attempt to dismiss the suit, the prince settled.

Still, the Andrew Problem is the gift that keeps on giving for the British royal family.

The Queen's second son, wrote the New York *Times*, settled with an alleged rape victim and while he "did not admit guilt in the settlement, he was forced to commend Virginia Giuffre, who accused him of raping her when she was a teenager, for her bravery in coming forward. He also agreed to pay her a sum that London newspapers reported to be more than $13 million."

Actually, the reported figure is closer to $16 million, with some of that believed to have come from Andrew's mother, the late Queen Elizabeth.

The headlines were fun, with this one representing a particularly merciless jab:

"Royal wrong'un pays out to sex victim he's never met. As you do," said the *Daily Star* (Andrew told the BBC in 2019 that he had "no recollection" of ever meeting Giuffre).

Where did the money come from to pay off Prince Andrew's accuser? There is speculation some came in the form of a loan from his brother then-Prince Charles, and the rest from his mother, but some wondered if any of the payoff money came from taxpayer money.

Postscript: Unsurprisingly, on June 19, 2022, The *Sunday Times* (UK) came out with another bullying story—this time saying the Buckingham Palace investigation into Meghan Markle's alleged bullying of staffers when she was a working royal has forced changes to the "policies and procedures" of the monarchy's HR department, but also that, conveniently, the findings were "buried" and will never see the light of day.

As Bot Sentinel's Christopher Bouzy—a well-known figure among Sussex fans who spends a lot of time fighting abuse and bullying on Twitter and identifying the worst offenders—Tweeted the day the *Sunday Times* story came out, "Why announce you are launching a probe into the Meghan Markle bullying claims, but refuse to release the findings of the probe? Seems like they didn't find anything, and they are too embarrassed to admit nothing was found."

That's certainly part of it. The other part is the obvious possibility there was never a probe to begin with.

In any case, wherever the money to pay Andrew's accuser came from, the fact it happened at all should be enough to see the thread and begin to pull it.

Paying off a credible woman who says she was raped by one of the senior royals is a slippery slope indeed.

CHAPTER 7

THE INVISIBLE CONTRACT

The royal family and the British media have been conspiring forever.

Prince Harry, who lived through his mother's vilification, divorce and tragic death, said it quite plainly:

"There is this invisible contract behind closed doors, behind the institution and UK tabloids," Harry said during the Oprah interview. "Well, to simplify it, it's a case of if you, as a family member, are willing to wine, dine, and give full access to these reporters, then you will get better press. I think everybody needs to have some compassion in that situation. There is a level of control by fear that has existed for generation."

"Who's controlling whom?" Oprah pressed.

"The institution survives based on that perception," Harry replied.

Meghan explained further: "There's a reason these tabloids have holiday parties at the palace. There is a construct at play there and because of the beginning of our relationship, they were so attacking and inciting so much racism, really, it changed the risk level because it wasn't just catty gossip. It was bringing out a part of people that was racist in how it was charged and that changed the threat; that changed the level of death threats, that changed everything." (Emphasis mine).

That this invisible contract exists is something upon which sources on both sides seem to agree.

Sources like Prince Harry himself on the family side.

Sources like me and my past journalism colleagues on the media side, who lived through and are still living by this invisible contract.

I remember remarking to a British journalist friend over a pint in London in the early 2000s that strapping young Prince William was still single, and wondering idly who might have her sights set on him, and my friend said, "But he's with Kate Middleton, isn't he?"

"He is?"

"Yes. We're just not supposed to write about her. They live together."

What?

I was covering hard news then, before I began taking on royal-related assignments, and I'd never once heard her name. No one I knew, especially back in the States, had ever heard of this Kate, an athletic brunette who lived off-campus with a bunch of guys.

The press wrote about her only in passing, with eu-phemisms and wink-winks, so that the casual royal watcher—especially outside of Britain—would never pick up that there was a romance there.

William the university student was not to be touched by the press nor their photographers.

That was the deal.

If it had been business as usual, paparazzi and young reporters posing as students would have infested the little town of St. Andrews, crawled through its pubs, its parties, its residence halls. But no. It was strictly hands off—except for the occasional feature that leaked out of the town, reported from a distance with scant details.

For example, on October 4, 2002, *Hello!* magazine ran a story hinting at a budding chemistry between the young blond prince: "St. Andrews University student Prince William is leaving the hall of residence where he's spent the last year in order to move into a luxury flat with three friends—and one of his new roomies is apparently a pretty 20-year-old brunette.

"Fellow History of Art classmate Kate Middleton will share the home with William, along with Fergus Boyd—a 21-year-old who was at Eton with the Prince—and one other student."

The palace confirmed to media that William had left his rowdy student housing at St. Andrews's St. Salvator's Hall in favor of private accommodation.

The article added, "William's friendship with Kate was revealed last April, when the young royal paid £200 for a VIP seat at a university charity fashion show in which the Berkshire beauty was modeling."

That "fashion show" was the infamous event at which young Kate Middleton wore a see-through skirt as a dress and worked the runway with a suitably sultry pout.

Which brings up another historical fact about the royal family: Conspiratorial commoners are at work outside it, as well.

Take Carole and Kate Middleton, the mother-daughter duo who have long been rumored to have made a point of thrusting Kate into the prince's orbit.

Prince William met Kate Middleton, the eldest child of commoners Carole and Michael, at the University of St. Andrews in Scotland—where many royal writers have claimed Kate enrolled specifically to pursue him.

A 2013 *Daily Mail* article titled "Kate Middleton: Duchess of Cambridge 'changed university to be close to Prince William'" explained that "The Duchess of Cambridge switched university and took a gap year to ensure she attended at the same time as Prince William."

Indeed, Kate had been accepted at Edinburgh University in 2000 but gave up her spot and applied at St. Andrews for the 2001 incoming class after it was publicly announced William would be attending that school.

According to Jasper Selwyn, the career adviser at Kate's boarding school (what Americans call high school), Marlborough College, she had ranked Edinburgh as her top choice and had a spot at her dream school.

"Kate's firm choice was Edinburgh and that was confirmed," he told royal biographer Katie Nicholl for her book Kate: The Future Queen.

Nicholl called Kate's choice to deep-six her golden-ticket acceptance at Edinburgh in favor of attempting to get into St. Andrews "bold," "risky," "sudden" and "out of character," and wrote, "It seemed every girl in America wanted to come to St. Andrews to search out the prince. Kate would have read the papers. She would have known that William was going and that there was every chance they could be in the same program at the same time if she got a place to study there."

Kate got herself in William's eyeline when they started as freshmen, and before long they were friends.

That began to change, the story goes, when William might have started looking at her in a different light after she strode the catwalk in a see-through dress-that-was-really-supposed-to-be-a-skirt, showing her underwear to the world (unclutch your pearls, it's fine) during the aforementioned college fashion show.

Let's look at some ways the royal family can pick and choose which stories they speak out about, which ones they might steer from courtiers briefing reporters from the shadows, and which they allow to proliferate without comment.

CHAPTER 8

THE DUCHESS OF TIGHTS

One could view this battle portrayed in the media about a wedding-related showdown as a way to pit two women against each other.

One could also see it as pitting one white English rose against one biracial American woman.

But if neither woman speaks about the incident after it happens, then what are you left with?

Duchess Meghan says she was told to stay silent about royal matters that ended up in the media—to stick to the longtime family ethos of "Never complain, never explain" (which we have already shown is a directive as outdated and phony as certain HRHs are).

Yet *someone* briefed at least one reporter about this tearful tights encounter between Meghan Markle and Kate Middleton at a delicate time when they would soon become sisters-in-law.

British royal reporter Camilla Tominey, who routinely falls afoul of the so-called "Sussex Squad"—a global movement of Meghan and Harry defenders and fans who routinely raise money for causes favored by the couple—was the first to report the story that Kate Middleton was driven to tears by Meghan over some tights while planning Meghan and Harry's wedding.

The story goes like this: Kate wanted Princess Charlotte to wear tights for her role as a bridesmaid because of the formality of the occasion; Meghan didn't think the little girl should have to. They also reportedly argued about hems on the girls' dresses.

Kate's waterworks reportedly ensued due to how frightfully mean Meghan was.

A story leaked after it happened. Was it Kate or Meghan who shared it?

Let's examine the facts: Who did the narrative favor? Who had something to gain from allowing it to bloom and thrive and grow?

It favored Kate. Someone associated with the palace clearly briefed Camilla Tominey.

That construct, we now know, has since been flipped on its head, and the truth is that Kate made Meghan cry with her harshness, the Duchess of Sussex later told Oprah.

This revelation that Kate wasn't so innocent took many months to emerge and sparked the viral social media hashtag #DuchessofTights, referencing how Kate actually (allegedly) made Meghan cry—and called out Kate and Kensington Palace for not correcting the false public narrative to reflect this, which was perhaps the bigger transgression.

Depressingly, Tights Gate lived on even into late 2022 and beyond, when royal reporter Valentine Low's book *Courtiers: The Hidden Power Behind the Crown* came out with claims that Markle was "obsessed" with the palace disputing whatever went on with Kate.

"The truth is that after the dress fitting, Meghan had become obsessed with trying to persuade the palace press office to put something out denying the story," Low writes. "[The palace] were equally adamant that it would be a serious mistake to start briefing about personal stories relating to differences between members of the Royal Family."

Let's take a closer look at this particular claim: ...*it would be a serious mistake to start briefing about personal stories relating to differences between members of the Royal Family.*

I'm sorry *what*? There are not enough pages available here to reveal how many stories quoting senior royal sources about "differences between members of the Royal Family" have run in the pages of British newspapers over the years.

Here's one example from 2020: This ran after it was revealed Harry and Meghan were leaving their roles as working royals in the UK and moving to North America.

Right-wing journalist Dan Wootton trumpeted this "exclusive" in *The Sun*:

"The failure to consult other Royals has triggered outrage. A senior source said: 'Their statement was not cleared with anyone. It breaks all protocol. This is a declaration of war on the family. There is fury over how they've done this without any thought for the implications for the institution. The Queen is deeply upset. **The Prince of Wales and Duke of Cambridge are incandescent with rage.** Courtiers can't believe it. There are so many unanswered questions but they've just up and done it without a thought for anyone else. The plan was there to discuss it and work out a way that works for everyone in the family.'"

British writer Catherine Mayer, author of heavy tomes including *Charles: The Heart of a King* who is plugged into the who's who of London society, has tried to explain a few times over the years what's going on:

"The racism towards Meghan was and is very real," Mayer wrote on Twitter. "The abuse directed to her is out of all proportion to anything she's supposed to have done or did. The timing of allegations and the sharing of information was of course not coincidental.

"That doesn't mean she's flawless. Nobody is."

Mayer, who coincidentally studied English literature at the University of Sussex, added, "The monstering of Meghan is part of a culture of misogyny and racism more often promoted than challenged by media."

In any case, no one from the British royal family has come forth to dispute the reporting in Valentine Low's book, which made international headlines for days in the autumn of 2022.

No one from the palace has offered a quote about it, anonymous or otherwise.

No publications, at this writing, have reported royal household briefings that dispute Low's reporting.

Never forget: They can affect the narrative when they want to.

They leak like the proverbial sieve. They have their say when they want to.

I'll say it again: *When they want to.*

Once again, this leads us back to parallels between Diana and Meghan.

When talking about the wedding tights kerfuffle, what Meghan said when she finally felt safe enough to share—only after she was safely away from the United Kingdom—was so eerily similar to sentiments Diana had uttered in the past it was as if she was channeling the beloved People's Princess:

"It was only once we were married, and everything started to really worsen that I came to understand that not only was I not being protected," Meghan said, adding that "they were willing to lie to protect other members of the family, but they weren't willing to tell the truth to protect me and my husband."

Now read the words of Princess Diana from 1995 in her interview with disgraced journalist Martin Bashir (it is now widely recognized the interview was fraudulently obtained but the words spoken within it portrayed Diana's authentic feelings):

When asked why she thought the royal family was conspiring to leak unflattering and/or false information about her to the British media, Diana replied,

"It was to make the public change their attitude towards me. It was, you know, if we are going to divorce, my husband would hold more cards than I would—it was very much a poker game, chess game."

Bashir: "Do you really believe that a campaign was being waged against you?"

Princess Di: "Yes I did, absolutely, yeah."

Bashir: "Why?"

Princess Di: "I was the separated wife of the Prince of Wales, I was a problem, full stop. Never happened before, what do we do with her?"

As Time magazine put it, "The royal press—called the Royal Rota—and the royal family share a symbiotic relationship, with the press reporting extensively on the family's events in exchange for access. Given the appetite for royal news in the U.K., the relationship has been lucrative for the media and important for the family in their attempts to maintain relevance and a connection with non-royals without sacrificing privacy."

I have been on assignment with various members of the royal rota. It's a bizarre relationship between them and the family to say the least.

The actual reporters, on a given day, are treated like vermin by the royals and the Firm. On other occasions, like unwanted guests at a wedding you still have to be polite to.

Sometimes the reporters truly believe they've struck up some sort of friendship with their royal sources.

They're usually wrong.

Who can forget Prince Charles's gritted teeth when he didn't know he was mic'ed, during a photocall in Klosters, Switzerland, on a skiing holiday in 2005?

"I hate doing this. Bloody people," now-King Charles III said through visibly gritted teeth. He then lasered in on the BBC's Nicholas Witchell and said, "I can't bear that man anyway. He's so awful, he really is. I hate these people."

They despise them, but they use the media best they can to keep their reputations intact.

Sure, it's not working too well lately, but that doesn't stop them from trying.

CHAPTER 9

A MONARCHY THAT WILL SLAY TO STAY

Drownings, beheadings, kidnappings, cover-ups.

These are just some of the methods used by British royals throughout history to advance their agenda or do away with inconvenient or out-of-favor people.

Take George, the Duke of Clarence, for example. He was born in Dublin in 1449, and his oldest brother happened to be Edward IV, who would become the first Yorkist king.

George was titled as Duke of Clarence in 1461, the day after his brother's coronation, at which point George became Edward's heir.

Ah, but being so close to power without actually having much of it got to George, according to some accounts.

As relations with his brother deteriorated, the duke eventually joined the Earl of Warwick in open rebellion, capturing and holding Edward prisoner for a time.

They had to let him go, though, and understandably, relations continued to worsen between George and Edward.

Finally, in February of 1478, when the king's brother George, Duke of Clarence, was only 28, he was executed and the story goes that King Edward ordered his brother drowned in a vat a malmsey wine.

We cannot, of course, ignore the brutality of Henry VIII.

Voted by historians in polls as the worst monarch in history and referred to by one as a "pathological monster," Henry was so desperate for a male heir to keep his family in power he had two of his own wives executed.

He was laser-focused on securing the future of the Tudor dynasty and when his wife Anne Boleyn failed to bear him a son, Anne was arrested in 1536 and taken to the Tower of London past the most notorious entrance, called Traitors Gate, and that May, she became the first queen of England to be executed.

Long after her death, Anne's daughter with Henry VII, Elizabeth, would become the subject of her own enduring conspiracy theory.

Elizabeth was born in 1533 and would become Elizabeth I. For many reasons too exhaustive to go into here, there have been rumors she was really a man.

Novelist Steve Berry in his book *The King's Deception* ratchets up the conspiracy theory that the monarch was male.

It sounds bananas if you haven't heard it before, but in the context of the turmoil of the times and the cruelty of Elizabeth I's father King Henry III, Berry and others make surprisingly convincing case that it quite possibly could have been another British royal conspiracy to cover up the truth.

It's only a matter of time until the Princes in the Tower case spawns its own true-crime podcast.

The vanishing of two young princes is one of the most enduring mysteries in British history.

In a harrowing turn of events that is still debated by historians to this day, the two boys, Edward, 12 and his little brother Richard, 9, were sent to the dreaded Tower of London—and were never seen again.

It all began in 1483 when the Wars of the Roses were raging. In the midst of chaos and turmoil, King Edward IV died under mysterious circumstances, leaving two young sons behind.

He was just 40 when he became ill with an unknown ailment that spring. He had the best medical care of the day, but even with top doctors treating him, Edward died within 10-12 days of falling ill at the Palace of Westminster.

Medieval aides and physicians struggled to come up with a cause of death, and the top rumors involved poisoning, possibly from wine given to him by the King of France. To this day, arsenic is the top culprit for those who believe the poisoning theory.

Some blame King Edward's penchant for indulging, which they say led him party so hard for so long that it killed him. One blogger reports some people were reaching so desperately for a cause of death that they claimed Edward IV died after "eating a salad after he had become overcome by heat (in April! in England!!)"

Whatever the cause, when the king died, his two sons with Elizabeth Woodville were left without a father at the tender ages of 12 and 9. Edward was his rightful heir, and became Edward V at the age of 12.

Upon his death Edward IV's brother, the Duke of Gloucester, who was the boys' uncle, became Lord Protector of Edward V, or what was known officially as "protector of the realm."

The Duke—who would soon become Richard III—immediately sent Edward to the Tower of London, and it wasn't long before his little brother Richard would follow.

This move, Richard said, was for "their protection."

The Duke declared himself King Richard III, and Edward and his brother were never seen again.

Historians continue to dig up clues even now, and every tidbit adds to the picture and can be used to bolster a given case for a preferred suspect.

Example: Though Shakespeare's play *Richard III* infused the cultural zeitgeist with a solid suspect, telling us the medieval monarch killed his nephews, some historians vehemently disagree.

"The key suspect is undoubtedly Richard III," an article in Edinburgh University's *Retrospect* journal acknowledges. It's true: the ruler had motive, means and opportunity.

But some experts caution not to wear blinders when naming suspects in the case.

"In more recent years, however, there has been a more sympathetic reading of Richard III. Modern sympathizers of Richard III have created an almost cult-like following of people rushing to defend the person termed the 'first victim of fake news' by the Richard III society's chair, and respected historian, Matt Lewis."

Lewis, indeed, argues that the murder of the nephews is most certainly not solved. Though the king clearly had motive, the historian points out "his actions do not suggest that he killed the princes…had Richard killed the princes, then he would have at least publicized the fact that they had died, in order to stop them from being a threat," the article goes on.

The obvious flaw in that claim is that if their death was publicized, there would be outrage and the boys would possibly be martyred.

Then again, argue some, that still wouldn't be enough to change history.

"They may have been cult-like in status, but they would have still been dead, and unable to launch a rebellion," the journal article points out.

Matt Lewis writes on his own blog about a "great misconception that the Tower of London was a locked and bolted prison, a dark place with a sinister character. That was not true until the Tudor era…the Tower was a functioning royal palace, a busy and bustling place where the Royal Treasury was frequently housed, Council meetings held and military provisions stockpiled."

With that in mind, it wouldn't necessarily be a given that Richard III sent the boys there to meet their untimely deaths.

Lewis, in fact, points to another suspect, a woman some have called the original medieval momager: Lady Margaret Beaufort.

She was known to have done everything possible to ensure her son (the Lancastrian heir) eventually ascended the throne.

(Remind you of any modern-day English royalty-adjacent moms?).

Anyway, Lewis makes his case in-depth on his blog.

He says, for example, there is "a clear indicator that Margaret Beaufort's work on her son's behalf in the late summer of 1483 was advanced, ran deep, was secret and relied on the death of the Princes in the Tower. It was Margaret who opened up a clandestine line of communication to [the young princes' mother] Elizabeth Woodville in sanctuary at Westminster Abbey. Margaret used her physician Lewis Caerleon, who posed as Elizabeth's physician, to pass messages between the two women."

Assuming the boys were actually murdered at all, he argues, this would give Margaret motive, means and opportunity. Richard III, along with the Duke of Buckingham, both remain viable suspects, too, Lewis added.

Interestingly, there have been two unidentified skeletons found in the Tower that some believe to be the brothers, but no one knows for sure. The remains were interred at Westminster Abbey.

The disappearance of the princes remains shrouded in mystery—but maybe not forever. An English historian whose research helped identify the remains of Richard III in 2012 also discovered the mitochondrial DNA (mtDNA) of the princes in the Tower.

This blockbuster discovery by Dr. John Ashdown-Hill MBE, who died in 2018, means it could be possible to prove whether the bones at Westminster Abbey are those of Edward V and his brother Richard.

Ashdown-Hill's findings were published posthumously in *The Mythology of the Princes in the Tower.*

He said that year, "It is generally believed that the boys' bones were found at the Tower of London in 1674 and were taken to Westminster Abbey where they remain. Those bones should be re-examined now to determine whether they are those of Edward and Richard."

Even more recently, a group of researchers have come up with an entirely different scenario for what happened to the young princes.

They point out that no evidence of Edward and Richard being murdered has ever been discovered, and revealed that a series of *Da Vinci Code*-style clues have made them suspect there is every possibility their eventual deaths were not due to homicide.

The Missing Princes Project, led by historian Philippa Langley, followed a paper trail including medieval documents that led them to Coldridge in Devon, England, where royal Yorkist symbols are carved into St. Matthew's Church.

It's possible, researchers say, that a deal was struck between the boys' mother and Richard III that allowed Edward to live his life under the fake name "John Evans," and in fact the remote church very well might hold to the 500-year-old royal "murder" mystery, according to lead researcher John Dike.

The historians suggest the secret messages prove that the deposed King Edward V was not murdered in the Tower of London, but lived a full life under the fake name in the Devon village.

"The idea of a missing prince lying low in Devon might appear fanciful at first," Dike has said, "but the discoveries inside this church in the middle of nowhere are extraordinary."

History showing Richard III as a cold-blooded, power-hungry murderer of his nephews was actually "propaganda" used in the war for the throne so many years ago, as some suspect, or whether he really did slay his nephews, one thing seems certain: The royal family was involved in the conspiracy to get the young princes out of the picture, whatever the motive and means were.

CHAPTER 10

A DEATH IN THE ROYAL FAMILY— AND A COVER-UP?

Prince George, the Duke of Kent, was the wild child of the staid royal family back in the 1920s.

One of his most famous liaisons was with a glamorous American socialite named Kiki Preston.

Often referred to as "the girl with the silver syringe" due to her drug use and willingness to shoot up in public, Kiki Preston was a fixture of high-society circles in Paris and New York City, and a relative of the prominent Vanderbilt and Whitney families.

Preston was part of the so-named The Happy Valley set, a community of mostly British expatriates living in Kenya who became legendary for their hedonistic lifestyle.

She met Prince George in the roaring twenties and, the story goes, lured him into a drug-fuelled lifestyle of partying all day and all night.

The wayward prince, who was already known as a partier himself and famously had an affair with playwright Noel Coward, grew addicted to morphine and cocaine.

The British royal family was horrified and panic-stricken over the relationship as well as George's ensuing drug addiction, and Edward, then the Prince of Wales, tried to drive a wedge between them.

When that didn't work, Edward eventually forced George to stop seeing her—and kicked Preston out of England entirely when she was visiting George in the summer of 1929.

The star-crossed lovers would run into each other after that, but Edward found creative ways to keep them apart.

George, who was also the Duke of Kent and a popular fellow in the United Kingdom known as "Georgie," later married a Greek woman called Marina and had three children with her.

And then, in 1942, with World War II raging, Prince George died mysteriously in a tragic plane crash.

We do know some facts about the incident. The RAF flying boat he was traveling in hit the side of a mountain in Scotland and killed all but one aboard when the craft went up in a jet-fueled fireball.

We know the aircraft, which was heading to Iceland for base inspections, took off from Invergordon, on the east coast of Scotland, at 1:10 p.m. on August 25, 1942.

Thirty minutes later, all but one of its passengers were dead.

Locals in the village of Dunbeath reported hearing an ear-splitting explosion. It was believed that, navigating through a wall of sea mist, the plane had lost its bearings and slammed into the side of Eagle's Rock.

So much else about the circumstances of that flight and subsequent crash are unknown.

Sensational claims made by royal journalist and biographer Christopher Wilson in 2021 make a case for a royal cover-up.

Prince George's loss was one of the most hard-hitting and well-known of World War II. The nation was in shock and mourning, and yet, "after a hastily arranged funeral held just four days later, no public memorial was erected in memory of him—no statue, no official biography, no charity bearing his name. He was airbrushed from history," Wilson wrote in the *Daily Mail*.

The inquiry was held in private, and the families of those killed on board weren't even allowed to hear the proceedings.

According to Wilson, helping to spawn endless ongoing conspiracy theories is the fact that the National Archives, the RAF Historical Branch, the Imperial War Museum and the Royal Archives at Windsor "all deny having possession of the key records relating to the death of George V's son and his fellow aviators."

Was George flying that day? Was he drunk?

Or, was it something else entirely that required a ring of silence around the crash?

Wilson writes that "the Establishment's connivance at a cover-up may well have been because the Prince had secretly…smuggled a woman lover on board the fatal flight."

Indeed, Wilson's research and interviews led him to believe there was a woman on board that day—which would have been illegal on that mission—and the only way she would have been allowed to fly was at the invitation of Prince George himself.

"A number of unanswered questions hang in the air to this day," Wilson writes. "The crash occurred at about 1:40 p.m., yet the Duke's brother, King George VI, holidaying not far away at Balmoral, was not informed until around 8:30 p.m., when a courtier interrupted a family dinner to break the news. Why was the tragedy kept from him? Was it because senior officers needed time to decide what to do with the 'extra person'?"

There are theories that persist to this day, but those in the royal family who might know the truth aren't talking.

In the end, both George and his former glamorous and troubled lover Kiki Preston would both suffer tragic and untimely demises.

In 1946, at the age of 48, Preston jumped to her death from her fifth-floor apartment in New York City.

CHAPTER 11

HOW FAR WILL A MODERN-DAY MONARCHY GO TO ENSURE ITS SURVIVAL?

Think these medieval machinations are a thing of the past? Think again.

When pushed against a wall, hereditary royals who live off the state and historically plundered assets have been known to perpetrate shocking crimes and solutions to ensure their survival.

While there is no suggestion the current royal family will be hanging people on the scaffold again, they are not above craftier, more subtle and hidden means of self-preservation.

Princess Diana's son Prince Harry drew a parallel between her life and ultimate fate in 1997, and that of his wife Meghan and her precarious situation in the present.

Harry's most pointedly shocking statement, perhaps, was this one:

"My biggest concern was history repeating itself—I've said that before on numerous occasions, very publicly," he told Oprah. "And what I was seeing was history repeating itself, but perhaps, or definitely, far more dangerous, because then you add race in, and you add social media in."

In case there was any doubt, in case people tried to parse and soften his words, Prince Harry said, "And when I talk about history repeating itself, I'm talking about my mother."

You heard it straight from the royal's mouth.

During the now-legendary Oprah interview, Prince Harry was blunt, frank and pulled no punches.

His wife was in danger—and had been for some time. She was being hounded and abused by the British media. Her mental health was suffering.

When they moved out of the UK, their royal protection was pulled. Harry's own father reportedly had a hand in pulling their royal protection security force, with the Firm whipping it away, the Sussexes say, with little or no notice.

Even though his family knew more than anyone how much danger the 5th in line for the British throne would be in without it.

If they didn't know, they wouldn't have round-the-clock royal protection for themselves. Yet they pulled it.

Harry and Meghan got out of Britain before the worst could happen.

"I was desperate," Harry told Oprah of the big split from the UK. "I went to all the places I thought I should go to ask for help; we both did, separately and together."

Harry continued, "When you can see something happening in the same kind of way, anybody would ask for help, ask for the system of which you are a part of—especially when you know there's a relationship there [with the press]—that they could help and share some truth or call the dogs off, whatever you want to call it."

Harry said he and Meghan received "no help at all."

He also commented on how his mother might feel about his and Meghan's decision to step away from what they viewed as a toxic situation in which Meghan claimed royal aides took her passport, driver's license and keys and kept hold of them while she was a working royal.

"I think [my mother] would feel very angry with how this has panned out and very sad," Harry said. "But ultimately, all she'd ever want is for us to be happy."

The prince had to take his case for added protection in the UK to the courts, and his legal team filed an application for a judicial review—which is a challenge in the High Court against the decision of a public body or government department—because of an incident over the summer (which I covered in *Harry & Meghan Vol. 2*).

A legal representative for Prince Harry said the legal claim was filed "to challenge the decision-making behind the security procedures, in the hopes that this could be re-evaluated for the obvious and necessary protection required."

Here is the problem: The protection Harry and his family need in the United Kingdom is protection money cannot buy. Any security teams or bodyguards he hires himself cannot, by British law, be armed.

Perhaps more important, Harry's team is privately run, and therefore not privy to known threats, plans or intel by bad actors who might be targeting the Prince. While the police will have a full dossier of threats made against his family's lives or well-being, the guards Harry hires can be reactive only.

They don't know which routes to avoid.

Which vehicles to look out for.

Which direction the threats might be coming from.

Harry isn't asking for police protection for him and his family because he's an entitled brat. It's because they all have targets on their backs and only official insiders within British law enforcement and government have access to those who might be planning harm on a given day.

Harry's team could drive him right into an ambush and never see it coming—and the ambush would know they are unarmed sitting ducks. It's not amusing, it's not safe, and it's not OK.

He and Meghan had already made the strong case that should not have to be made in the first place: He and his children were born into the royal life. They did not choose it nor court the publicity.

That Harry is a living, breathing piece of history is no fault of his own.

So far, those pleas had fallen on deaf ears in his home country.

Here's what we're left with: The royal family has made it clear they do not like what Harry and Meghan did or how they did it.

They've come out with "bullying" claims about Meghan spanning years now.

And then they pull Harry, Meghan, Archie and Lilibet's security services while in Harry's native United Kingdom.

And then they make Harry fight to get it back, at his own expense.

Think about that: His family has forced him to fight to protect himself, his wife and his children.

Taking the next leap in logic is not a stretch.

Something doesn't smell right.

Never underestimate how far any living organism, even one comprised will go in a bid for self-preservation.

It's in our DNA, after all.

"All biological organisms are subject to the survival instinct, which is thus the potent biological cause of inter-group aggression. Groups compete for territory and see other groups as a threat," wrote Nevin Hughes-Jones in his abstract for his journal article *Inter-Group Aggression: The Multi-Individual Organism and the Survival Instinct.*

The players will change, but the game remains the same.

On September 22, 2022, the first day of autumn in the Northern Hemisphere, headlines about a "CONSPIRACY!" within the royal family rocked the UK.

The gist of the shocking story was that back in the day, Prince Andrew secretly plotted with his ex-wife Sarah "Fergie" Ferguson to prevent Charles from becoming King—a move that, if successful, would allow Prince William to take the throne with the Duke of York (Andrew) as Regent.

These dramatic claims are in Angela Levin's latest biography about Camilla Parker-Bowles, who is now Queen Consort.

Levin alleges that Prince Andrew "lobbied" Queen Elizabeth II to get in on the plan, and furthermore campaigned against Charles marrying Camilla because she was apparently not trustworthy.

Levin also writes that Prince Andrew was "very nasty" to Camilla and conspired with Princess Diana to prevent Prince Charles from becoming King.

Under Andrew's alleged plan, William would have been next in line for the throne with Charles pushed out and Andrew made Regent if the Queen had died before William turned 18.

In years gone by, this kind of treasonous talk could render some terrifying consequences.

One wonders if, upon reading the headlines in 2022, Prince Andrew feared execution by drowning in a vat of wine, a fate suffered by one of his princely predecessors by the hand of his brother the King, as we discussed earlier.

All jokes aside, see how the palaces use the invisible contract to get their side of the story out?

They haven't disputed the claims in this book, which means Camilla is tacitly approving these claims, which also target our beloved Princess Di, whose husband Camilla cheated with.

Camilla, after all, was the third person in Charles and Diana's marriage—the marriage Diana famously called "a bit crowded" due to Camilla having an affair with her husband.

Anyway, things were looking a bit scandalous for the royals that week.

And then #KingCharlestheCruel started trending on Twitter, partly because the new King Charles III still hadn't let on whether he'd decided to let his son Harry's children, whose titles automatically became Princess Lilibet and Prince Archie upon Queen Elizabeth II's death, keep those new titles.

Within days, there was another leak about the monarch's machinations.

A friend of King Charles III told the *Mail on Sunday* that basically, the palaces continue to freak out about what might be in Prince Harry's upcoming memoir.

The king's friend told the newspaper, "The question inside the Palace is, 'Can the book be stopped?' It may be that even Harry can't stop it at this stage but the feeling at the very top is that there's no good that can come of airing grievances in public."

"Lawyers to the Royal Family at the firm Harbottle and Lewis are expected to be on standby to read the book when it comes out," the article added.

It feels a bit like everyone in the world except senior British royals realize we're past the point of no return.

It's happening, and there's nothing they can do about it.

There are many questions left hanging surrounding many members of the royal family, and you can certainly guess what topics the royals are afraid to address.

One is, which family member questioned what Archie's skin color might be before he was born? (Another topic covered well in my other books).

Another question remains about Harry and Meghan's original night nurse for their first child, Archie.

Royal biographer Omid Scobie revealed details about the moment the couple chose to keep private.

"After Archie's arrival, Harry and Meghan wanted some help to establish a sleep pattern. They hired a night nanny," Omid revealed. "Whilst I can't go into someone else's employment details for legal reasons, it was an incident on one of the first nights that put the couple off from having a night nurse."

Omid went on to add that the 'incident' remains a private issue, even to those close to the Duke and Duchess of Sussex.

"Very few people know the real story behind it," he added.

Anything we say now about the nanny's dismissal will be speculation, so we must say nothing, other than to pose the question and listen out for any revelations to come.

And then, of course, there is the question that has piqued the interest of and stoked the fires of suspicion in Sussex fans and royal watchers all across social media for years:

How did Meghan's dog, a sweet little Beagle called Guy, break two legs not long after Meghan arrived to live permanently with Harry in the UK? The reports came out at the time and said she was beside herself, that Guy was being looked after by the best veterinarians, but very little else was revealed.

Some conspiracy theorists wonder…how could something that traumatic have happened? And why?

The façade of a benign and necessary sovereignty was already unraveling before the queen's death.

Without her, Charles's cash-for-honors scandal and Andrew's Epstein connections and rape accusations, plus Harry and Meghan's outcast status along with a "bullying" investigation that went nowhere, all of it has torn through the family fabric, poking holes in the gauzy fairy-tale curtain the royal family lived behind for much of Elizabeth II's 70-year reign.

How far would the institution of the British monarchy go to ensure its own survival? What would they sacrifice, or maybe more to the point, whom?

Perhaps a better question: If King Charles III saw his own teetering popularity sink further and further (admittedly a big if) so much that it began to drag the entire institution and Royal Household down, would he step aside to give William a chance to resurrect any kind of good will toward the crown? Is it even worth considering?

I'm not so sure.

Does Charles seem the type to make a sacrifice like that?

There are signs the monarchy will have to fight harder than it has in decades for its own survival.

Charles has by no means taken the throne while enjoying instant popularity.

He will not have an easy time of his reign coming onstage after his popular mother, historians and experts say.

Veteran royal biographer Clive Irving, in his book *The Last Queen*, suggests Charles and William, who would be Charles's direct heir, must step lightly and truly pay attention to their subjects in a winter of much discontent and the infamous #CostofLivingCrisis to keep the monarchy alive now that the queen is dead.

There are those who believe Queen Elizabeth II is the sole reason the monarchy still exists in the year 2022.

"She prolonged the life of the monarchy far longer than it otherwise would have been prolonged," Irving has said, adding that, "I think there's a really real risk that if Charles does succeed her that the monarchy will go over a cliff very fast.

"This question of the survival of the monarchy hasn't really arisen since the time of [Edward VIII's] abdication, but it will come up as a real smack in the face. She's enjoyed such a command of the role that the whole idea of abolition or republicanism has been beyond reality."

As of 2022, polls show that supporters of the Crown are a healthy majority of the British population, but that doesn't tell the full story nor account for one alarming statistic: Among the 18-to 24-year-old crowd, a full 40 percent wanted to abolish the monarchy compared to 37 percent who supported continuing with it.

More to the point, the percentage of those wanting to end the monarchy has continued to grow steadily over the years.

Graham Smith, chief executive of anti-monarchy pressure group Republic, said to *Newsweek*: "When looked at alongside other polls in recent years, it appears support for the monarchy is on a slow puncture."

As royal biographer Catherine Mayer points out, "The past years—the Meghan-and-Harry years, the Andrew-and-Jeffrey-Epstein years, the cash-for-honors-and-access years, the fragmenting-and-fracturing-of-family years—have hit the institution like a wrecking ball."

Mayer says Charles certainly has his fans and admirers, but also offers a caveat: "He remains, however, a polarizing figure trying to navigate an increasingly polarized world. The primary role of a head of state is to unify. This could be a bumpy ride."

A ride with bumps made of question marks, suspicion and secret agendas that might never see the light of day.

There are still questions left unanswered in the search for the truth about what really goes on in the Royal Household, the Firm, and the family. They include:

- Where is the Fiat?
- Will Diana's fans the world over, for generations to come, ever truly believe her death in a car crash was a tragic accident?
- Who broke Meghan's dog's legs, or how did they get broken?
- What is the story behind the night nurse who was fired for "unprofessional" behavior?
- Where did the money for Prince Andrew to pay off his rape accuser come from?
- Who brought up discussions about what then-unborn Archie's skin color might be?

One or more of these questions might be answered in the history books one day or, like many royal conspiracies in long-ago centuries, they might remain intriguing mysteries forevermore.

Watch this space. Stay tuned.

We'll continue to investigate and write about the royals and what really goes on within the Firm for as long as the monarchy lives off taxpayer money.

How long that will be remains to be seen.

***

OTHER TITLES FROM ONE MOMENT BOOKS

For more on the British media and Meghan, the Duchess of Sussex, read the #1 New Release on Amazon:

MEGHAN KILLED THE QUEEN: The British media's obsession with blaming the Duchess of Sussex for everything by Rose Hanes

Other titles by author Courtney Hargrove

#1 Bestseller on Amazon:

LONDON BRIDGE IS DOWN: The British government and royal family's secret plans to manage chaos and succession upon the death of Queen Elizabeth II

#1 New Releases on Amazon:

HARRY & MEGHAN VOL. 1: Rocking the monarchy, settling in California & how dare they be happy

HARRY & MEGHAN VOL. 2: A New American Royal Family Takes Their Place in History

THE SPLIT: Why are Prince William and Kate separating from their London home?

***

TRY A SAMPLE OF "THE SPLIT" BY COURTNEY HARGROVE:

THE SPLIT

Introduction: Where's William?

On August 21, 2022, Kate Middleton, the Duchess of Cambridge, boarded a plane destined for Inverness, Scotland.

With Kate on the commercial flight were two of her and Prince William's children, Princess Charlotte and Prince Louis, along with the family's live-in nanny Maria Borallo.

Prince William was nowhere to be seen.

Buffered by royal protection officers surrounding them in economy seating during the short flight, Kate was seen grabbing an iPad for seven-year-old Charlotte and smiling at a passenger who caught her eye.

Upon landing in Scotland, the royal entourage were escorted off the plane. Kate, her dark sunglasses hiding any expression and a long skirt swishing around her legs, strolled across the tarmac holding Charlotte's hand.

Before any other passengers were allowed to leave their seats, Kate, the children and their entourage slid into waiting SUVs standing by to whisk them to the queen's Balmoral estate, according to a passenger who reported back about the trip and took a quick video of the Cambridge family's departure.

The journey was unremarkable for the three royals—except for one thing.

There was a glaring, unavoidable question that sprung immediately to mind and clogged social media feeds and comment sections within hours:

Where was William? And what about Prince George?

Kate and the gang were traveling to a last-gasp summer holiday with the queen at their massive Scotland estate, Balmoral, and presumably William and George could be expected to be part of the family gathering, too.

But why were Kate and William apart for their travels again?

This was, in fact, the latest in a series of trips and commutes the couple had undertaken separately in recent months.

Kensington Palace doesn't comment on these sorts of things, and no explanation was forthcoming from their camp for the differing travel plans that day.

But the palace did have an announcement forthcoming, one the press and royal fans had been expecting for some time.

They shared the news the following day.

On August 22, Kensington Palace released a short missive on royal letterhead making official the murmurings that had been simmering in the media for months: Prince William and Kate were separating from their lives at the London palace and moving with George, Charlotte and Louis to Adelaide Cottage in Windsor.

All three children have waved goodbye to their London-based schools and are attending the prestigious $25,000-a-year Lambrook School in the county of Berkshire, where Kate's family of origin—parents Carole and Michael and siblings Pippa and James—all live now.

There is no denying it is a significant shift in the royal family. For Prince William and Kate Middleton, the Duke and Duchess of Cambridge, to separate rather abruptly from their old lives is no small thing.

They are leaving Kensington Palace in London and moving to the sleepier town of Windsor, where Queen Elizabeth reigns from her quarters at Windsor Castle.

This is a notable moment within a shaky monarchy in which senior royals are dwindling fast: Prince Philip recently died, Prince Harry left for California, and accused rapist Prince Andrew was disgraced out of his working-royal role (he denied all charges and settled with his accuser), for starters.

William is a presumed future king, and when he married commoner Kate Middleton in 2011 it was assumed she would be by his side as queen consort when the time came.

Why are they moving to a new home base now? Why uproot their marital home shortly after spending some $5.4 million in British taxpayer money and thousands of dollars of their own cash to fix up the old Kensington Palace apartment, after offering assurances that the changes were needed because the place was a "forever home?"

Should we extrapolate anything from the fact Kate is moving to the same county as her parents and siblings, a quieter place where the Cambridge family's back-and-forths between homes would be less visible than, say, driving along the Kensington High Street?

As keen royal observers and top journalists wonder aloud on social media whether all is well in the Cambridge marriage, it begs the question what this move might mean to the future of the monarchy.

A split this big within a royal family fighting for survival could distract from Prince Charles's smooth transition to King Charles.

It could push forward a tipping point; it could be the proverbial straw that broke the poor old camel's back.

Veteran royal biographer Clive Irving, in his book The Last Queen, suggests Charles and William must step lightly and will need to be ultra careful—and will likely need a dose of luck—to keep the monarchy alive when Queen Elizabeth, now 96, dies.

Indeed, there are many watching who wonder what a monarchy under King Charles would look like, and whether it could survive for long.

There are those who believe Queen Elizabeth is the sole reason the monarchy still exists in the year 2022.

"She prolonged the life of the monarchy far longer than it otherwise would have been prolonged," Irving has said, adding that, "I think there's a really real risk that if Charles does succeed her that the monarchy will go over a cliff very fast.

"This question of the survival of the monarchy hasn't really arisen since the time of [Edward VIII's] abdication, but it will come up as a real smack in the face. She's enjoyed such a command of the role that the whole idea of abolition or republicanism has been beyond reality."

The question is, even if the monarchy survives a relic like Charles, would it survive William, who even at his young age of 40 is seen by some as increasingly out-of-touch-before-his-time?

And what if—hypothetically speaking—he was no longer married when it was his turn to ascend the throne?

History has shown there is no simple answer, no easy way out, when there is a split between senior members of the royal family.

While there is no suggestion William and Kate will ever split, nor that there is any problem at all within their marriage, the royal family has had some history-making divorces that shook the very foundation of the monarchy.

One wonders what would happen if there was ever another one, though there is no sign that is on the cards for any married British royals.

For now, it is enough of an intriguing question to examine why the Cambridges are making such a big move, and how that is affecting the perception of them among British subjects and royal fans the world over.

1

The Split, Part I

"MAKING THE BEST OF IT: After the recent Sturm and Drang, the rumors and suspicions and angry rebellion, the Prince and Princess's once fairy-tale marriage is entering a new phase—one of dutiful accommodation. Has [she] bit the bullet? Or is she just biding her time?"

—a *Vanity Fair* magazine headline

Can you guess which senior British royal couple the headline above is about?

If you're a longtime watcher of all things royal, you've probably already conjured the correct answer.

The article that ran under this headline goes on to explain that the royal wife's recent birthday "…brought accolades from all sections of the British press for 'star quality' and 'unassuming charm:' she is, they said, 'the best thing to happen to the Royals . . . the feminine ideal.' Her new composure is hard won, and stems from her decision to do as royal women so often have, and make the best of a cool marriage instead of fighting it."

Have you guessed yet?

When you're part of one of the most-watched, most fascinating and most gossiped-about couples on earth, it's hard to truly hide the signs of discord within a union.

There are always signs.

When a British royal couple is on the verge of separating, maybe the future king and his pretty wife, who is also the mother of his adorable young children, are cool to each other in public.

Maybe she visibly flinches when he deigns to get near her or brush her shoulder with his hand at a public appearance. They rarely make eye contact, if ever.

We are, of course, speaking about Prince Charles and Princess Diana in the 1980s, when they began dating and became engaged after seeing each other a total of about a dozen times.

Those of us who were old enough to understand what was happening when Charles and Diana announced their separation after such fairy-tale beginnings recall the shock of these kinds of announcements all too well.

All the history-based shows and movies out there now, such as The Crown (Netflix), Spencer starring Kristen Stewart, and the well-received HBO documentary The Princess, are teaching a new generation about the poisonous way in which the monarchy sometimes operates and how it can destroy the people within it.

But those of us who watched the bitter split between Charles and Di unfold in real-time, when it was reality and not presented as a historical reimagining, have it seared into our memories.

It's a sensory experience for us; we can reach out and touch the nineties, recall Prince Charles's coldness, feel the claustrophobia of Diana as she was cornered by packs of British press and photographers while her marriage disintegrated in front of the world.

It was almost unbelievable to witness it in real time: Prince Charles, the man who was next in line for the throne, the future king, and his presumed future queen consort and the mother of their two adorable children, were splitting up.

How could that be?

Ah, but the signs were there. They'd been there all along.

The media and the general public speculated.

Headlines hinted.

Still, no one wanted to believe the fairy tale truly would end with such a dramatic, bitter severing.

Royal fans around the globe could barely fathom what a split in the marriage of next in line for the throne that would truly look like. It was too huge to contemplate.

It was difficult to accept even though these kinds of separations are not unusual. Major splits in monarchies and aristocracies have occurred throughout history, as have chilly marriages-turned-cool-arrangements for appearances' sake while one or both people carry on affairs or full-fledged relationships on the side.

At one publication I used to work for (there have been a handful of different ones internationally) we often knew from close sources that high-profile couples were separated and were living apart before the general public had a clue.

But we never reported a break-up until a split was made official and public by the couple or their representatives.

It's a dangerous game to do otherwise. Putting aside reasons of decency—after all, look at the media timeline we exist in now; decency is rarely a consideration—a publication or author cannot predict what the heart will do.

Perhaps a pair who seem irreparably shattered might reconcile. Perhaps they want to try living for years as a couple in name only for the children, or for some other reason, and that is still a marriage, and it remains their business alone.

No, at any reputable publication, you wait until the couple announces when and how they are going their separate ways. They don't owe us an explanation, of course, but pressure on famous couples is intense and their hand is usually forced by speculation and rabid packs of paparazzi.

We don't know what goes on inside someone else's intimate relationship, no matter how much certain editors and reporters try to convince you they do.

Back at that same publication I worked for, we used to have a saying:

A couple will announce they have split up when one of them falls in love with someone else.

This could mean a few things: One member of the couple falls in love with someone else who they want to be seen publicly with; one falls in love with someone else who refuses to be a side piece and demands to be the number-one monogamous partner; or one in the couple is caught red-handed cheating with an outside person and their spouse is never going to forgive them.

*(Sometimes this last factor is hastened along by unrelenting rumors and press reports, persistent social media hashtags and sporadic blue-check reporters and royal commentators Tweeting about a member of the royal family cheating, citing intel they swear is based on rock-solid reporting from the family's inner circle.

In mid-August 2022, for example, it happened yet again, these pesky, persistent rumors about a member of a royal couple. This time the one making the rounds was from a person claiming to be a BBC reporter.

This person mentioned old cheating rumors and started some new ones we hadn't heard about yet with a woman whose name we don't know. And so the ripples of suggestion become tsunamis and the mumbles become shouts until they can no longer be swept under the carpet).

Unless and until one of the above things occurs, famous couples can stagger along for as many years as suits them in any kind of partnership that suits them.

Until then, everything can be covered up, hidden, kept private, hammered out between the two people inside the marriage.

This has happened more than once inside the House of Windsor.

Still, try as they have over the centuries to "never complain, never explain," and to remain utterly discreet and beyond reproach, these messy events have a way of leaking out.

And then the leak is set aflame by worldwide attention, and media lights the match, and it becomes an explosion.

FOR MORE, VISIT COURTNEY HARGROVE'S
AMAZON PAGE

****